# UNFORGETTABLE
# ANCIENT SITES

# UNFORGETTABLE
# ANCIENT SITES

CHARTWELL
BOOKS

Copyright © 2017 BlueRed Press Ltd

This edition published in 2018 by Chartwell Books,
an imprint of The Quarto Group
142 West 36th Street, 4th Floor
New York, NY, 10018, USA
T (212) 779-4972 F (212) 779-6058
www.QuartoKnows.com

Produced by BlueRed Press Ltd

Chartwell titles are also available at discount for retail, wholesale, promotional, and bulk purchase. For details, contact the Special Sales Manager by email at specialsales@quarto.com or by mail at The Quarto Group, Attn: Special Sales Manager, 401 Second Avenue North, Suite 310, Minneapolis, MN 55401, USA.

ISBN-13: 978-0-7858-3640-7

10 9 8 7 6 5 4 3 2 1

Author Martin Derrick

Printed in China

# CONTENTS

# INTRODUCTION

HUMAN HISTORY IS SUCH AN EVERYDAY PART OF OUR LIFE THAT FEW OF US EVEN NOTICE ITS PRESENCE. Some people live in houses as old as, or older than, Peru's fabled fifteenth-century Machu Picchu, or alongside churches, chateaux, and other architectural achievements to rival those of Ancient Rome. We walk along streets lined with buildings dating back hundreds of years, and gather in the same public squares, theaters, and restaurants as our great-great-grandparents, and unwittingly walk over incredible engineering works of previous generations deep beneath our feet. While thinking ourselves modern, we live and walk through the marvels of the past every day and rarely ask what the structures our ancestors left might tell us of history.

Yet around the world are artifacts and monuments we cannot ignore so easily: monuments with the power to make us stop and wonder. These are places that continue to fire our imaginations long after their builders have been forgotten. Some are profoundly enigmatic, seemingly offering the secrets of ages past if only we knew how to decode them. Others, like Rome's Colosseum, offer little in the way of mystery. Their history is well documented by contemporary sources as well as more recent research. Instead, their power lies in an ability to jolt us out of our daily lives and into the past. To stand in the Colosseum today is to hear the distant echoes of brutal combat and the howls of a bloodthirsty mob, surrounded by Rome's dazzling power translated into elegant architecture. We imagine what it would have been like to live in those times and if we, too, would have enjoyed the spectacle of prisoners being torn apart by wild beasts.

Such places work a powerful magic on the human imagination; a power that increases when mysteries and enigmas surround a monument. For example, hundreds of books have been written about the Great Pyramid of Giza since the days of the Greek historian Herodotus, who visited the site more almost 2,500 years ago. Yet the pyramid still defies a complete and satisfactory explanation. To date no one has come up with a good reason as to why the design of the Great Pyramid incorporates numbers connected to astronomy—numbers that appear again and again in ancient mythologies around the world. To take just one example, as discussed in *Hamlet's Mill*, by Giorgio de Santillana and Hertha von Dechend, the numbers 432,000 or 43,200 or 4,320 are repeatedly found in myths from Scandinavia to India, as well as in the architecture of other monuments. In astronomical terms, it is a "precessional number," related to the movement of the stars over many thousands of years. Writers such as the best-selling Graham Hancock have asked whether it can be simple coincidence that the dimensions of the Great Pyramid of Giza reflect the dimensions of the Earth on a scale of 1:43,200. That is,

multiplying the perimeter of the pyramid by the "sacred" number 43,200 gives a measurement for the circumference of the Earth accurate to within one percent!

Other mysteries—a few of which we will explore—surround more of the monuments we are going to visit. Why do Machu Picchu, the Great Pyramid, Persepolis, Angkor Wat, Easter Island and its moai, and many more ancient monuments all stand in a single line around the circumference of the Earth? Why did the ancient Olmec people of Mexico leave behind giant sculptures that clearly depict Africans when no African is thought to have set foot on the American continent until well after Columbus's famous "discovery" of America? Who built Stonehenge and for what purpose? Such questions have long been asked, and it is up to the reader to decide whether they deserve further attention. What is beyond question is that many ancient monuments continue to act as mysterious mines of information about human history. New technology and better archaeological practice at many of these sites go hand in hand to rewrite our ideas of the past. To give one small example, analysis of the bones of gladiators found at Ephesus

*Left:* The carved head of a serpent watches over the central pyramid at Chichen Itza, where human sacrifices were made to the feathered serpent god, Kukulkan.

*Below:* A magnificent panoramic view over the upper and lower levels of the Incan city Machu Picchu.

suggests they ate a vegetarian diet rich in carbohydrates in order to gain weight. Far from being the lean, muscular combatants depicted in movies like *Gladiator*, it is possible that these fighters actively tried to gain as much fat as possible in order to protect their sensitive blood vessels and internal organs from blows they would inevitably receive in the arena.

Colossal or small, known or mysterious, local or foreign, the places in this book connect us with our most distant ancestors in much the same way that they attempted to connect to their own dead: through imagination and the preservation of knowledge. Today, few of us engage in ancestor worship, but we instinctively despair at the terrorist destruction of historic sites, and major archaeological finds continue to make front-page news. In fact the world's ancient monuments regularly draw bigger crowds than popular theme parks. Books exploring the mysteries of the ancient world and offering new theories constantly make the bestseller lists. In a very real sense, the world's ancient monuments help us to venerate our ancestors. Their presence creates a chain that tethers us to our most distant and deepest roots and provides a profound understanding of who we really are. Equally,

their mysteries enthrall all of us. What might solving them reveal about humankind?

Whether as simple as animal paintings made by our most distant ancestors or as vast an undertaking as a palace complex raised on an inaccessible peak, the ancient monuments in this book are truly unforgettable. They are places that spark the imagination and force us to stop and consider humanity's journey through history. They pull us back into a past that is often completely alien to our own times but also curiously similar. Perhaps, we ask, in spite of all our technology, we have not changed very much at all over the years. We still look up into the night sky and marvel at the stars, after all— we just do it with space telescopes now. And, like the builders of the ancient monuments, some humans still strain their resources to raise massive structures in honor of their gods, or engage in ambitious feats of engineering, and make art they hope will inform future generations about who they were. Others simply work on building sites, like people from all over the world in every generation from the dawn of humanity, making small contributions to structures that might enchant future generations.

## UNESCO World Heritage Site Nomination Process and Criteria

There is a four-stage nomination process for a site to gain UNESCO World Heritage status. In the first instance countries list their important natural and cultural heritage sites; this is the Tentative List. Countries can then submit a Nomination File to the World Heritage Centre for review. The nominated site is then appraised by the World Heritage Convention: the International Council on Monuments and Sites (ICOMOS), the International Union for Conservation of Nature (IUCN) and the International Centre for the Study of the Preservation and Restoration of Cultural Property (ICCROM). The final stage of the process is the annual meeting of the intergovernmental World Heritage Committee, which makes the final decision on the sites that will be inscribed on the World Heritage List.

UNESCO states that for a site to be included on the World Heritage List it *"must be of outstanding universal value and meet at least one out of ten selection criteria."* These criteria are listed in the accompanying panel.

Prior to 2005 the ten criteria were divided into two categories;
—cultural criteria (of which there were six)
—and natural criteria (of which there were four).
Since 2005 there has been just the one set of ten criteria.

*Left:* Hundreds of thousands of people are thought to have died in the arena of the Colosseum. Today, it is lit up in gold at night whenever a death sentence is commuted anywhere around the world.

### UNESCO SELECTION CRITERIA

(i)   To represent a masterpiece of human creative genius.

(ii)  To exhibit an important interchange of human values, over a span of time or within a cultural area of the world, on developments in architecture or technology, monumental arts, town-planning or landscape design.

(iii) To bear a unique or at least exceptional testimony to a cultural tradition or to a civilization which is living or which has disappeared.

(iv)  To be an outstanding example of a type of building, architectural or technological ensemble or landscape which illustrates (a) significant stage(s) in human history.

(v)   To be an outstanding example of a traditional human settlement, land-use, or sea-use which is representative of a culture (or cultures), or human interaction with the environment especially when it has become vulnerable under the impact of irreversible change.

(vi)  To be directly or tangibly associated with events or living traditions, with ideas, or with beliefs, with artistic and literary works of outstanding universal significance. (The Committee considers that this criterion should preferably be used in conjunction with other criteria).

(vii) To contain superlative natural phenomena or areas of exceptional natural beauty and aesthetic importance.

(viii) To be outstanding examples representing major stages of Earth's history, including the record of life, significant on-going geological processes in the development of landforms, or significant geomorphic or physiographic features.

(ix)  To be outstanding examples representing significant on-going ecological and biological processes in the evolution and development of terrestrial, fresh water, coastal and marine ecosystems and communities of plants and animals.

(x)   To contain the most important and significant natural habitats for in-situ conservation of biological diversity, including those containing threatened species of outstanding universal value from the point of view of science or conservation.

# EUROPE

# KNOSSOS
## CRETE

*Today, Knossos stands as a reminder that sometimes myth becomes reality.*
*With this single dramatic find our idea of history had to be radically revised.*

CELEBRATED IN THE POETRY OF HOMER AND STEEPED IN LEGENDS OF GODS and bull-headed monsters, the ancient Minoan capital of Knossos is considered to be Europe's oldest city. Here, built in layers one on top of the other, are the remains of buildings that date back to the Neolithic era, as long ago as 7,000 BCE. Over millennia, the ancient Minoans—a seafaring and trading folk with a sophisticated artistic heritage—built progressively grander and more elaborate complexes over older structures that had been destroyed by earthquakes or warfare. The last—and greatest—was a truly labyrinthine building, though hardly the dark maze where Theseus is said to have hunted the Minotaur. Instead, it was light, elegant, and decorated with beautiful frescoes. Historically reported to have been designed by the fabled Daedalus, myths tell us that the architect and his son, Icarus, were later imprisoned by King Minos and escaped by making wings so they could fly away. Failing to heed his father's warnings Icarus flew too close to the sun, which melted the wax in his wings and caused him to plummet to his death.

*Right*: The remains of Knossos Palace have been partially restored by the British archaeologist Arthur Evans in the early twentieth century.

*Below*: The throne in the Throne Hall is original, but the decoration is the product of Arthur Evans's imagination.

Whoever designed it, the ruined palace complex that seduces visitors today is undoubtedly a masterpiece of architecture and design. Dating to around 1700 BCE, it was the last of a succession of buildings on the site that was finally abandoned around 1375 BCE. Considered to be a purely mythical city for centuries, it was rediscovered in 1878 by Minos Kalokairinos and excavated in 1900 by the British archaeologist Arthur Evans, who subsequently built partial reconstructions of some of the buildings. Although opinion is divided on how accurately his work represents the ancient palace, it is widely agreed that it at least gives a general sense of how the buildings would have looked.

What remains of the Minoan city speaks of a joyous, exuberant, flamboyant people with a rich culture and refined tastes. At its height the ancient city would have supported a population of about 100,000 and covered an area of about 10 square kilometers (3.9 square miles). The palace complex alone is vast, occupying 14,000 square meters (150,000 square feet), and when built featured fountains and bathing areas, courtyards, banqueting halls, and shrines hidden among its complicated warren of brightly painted rooms. Other buildings include a smaller palace, a royal villa, and a house for the high priest (with its own altar) as well as a tomb.

**Site information:**

| | |
|---|---|
| **Location:** | Heraklion, Crete, Greece |
| **Type of structure:** | City and palace complex |
| **Area:** | 10 square kilometers (3.9 square miles) |
| **Completed:** | c. 1700 BCE (on a site that dates back to c. 7000 BCE) |

**Date of Inscription as a UNESCO World Heritage Site:** Submitted by Greece to the UNESCO "tentative list" in 2014

**UNESCO Criteria:** (ii) (iii) (vi)

*Right*: Unlike the fresco in the Throne Hall, the Dolphin Fresco was painstakingly restored from tiny original fragments though the artist was forced to use his imagination.

*Below*: A panoramic view of the ruins of Knossos—Europe's oldest city.

# THE ACROPOLIS
## GREECE

*Properly known as the Acropolis of Athens, the site derives its name from the Greek* akron, *meaning highest place, and* polis *(city). Acropolis, therefore, simply means: the highest point of the city.*

THERE ARE MANY ACROPOLEIS ACROSS THE ANCIENT GREEK WORLD, though the Athenian acropolis easily outshines them all, to the extent that it has become known simply as The Acropolis.

Archaeological evidence suggests that the rocky outcrop standing over modern Athens was significant to the area's earliest inhabitants and has been in constant use as a religious and residential site for about 5,000 years. Around 570 BCE a temple to Athena (the city's patron goddess) was raised here, followed by another temple about fifty years later. In 480 BCE, however, Athens was attacked by a Persian army and the temples of the ancient Acropolis were destroyed. Their remains would later be used to construct the site's curtain walls, while relics and statues were simply thrown into pits (forming a treasure trove waiting to be unearthed by later archaeologists). By around 461 BCE, however, the Persian threat had receded and Athens had a new leader—Pericles

(c. 495–429 BCE): a general, statesman, popular orator, and "the first citizen of Athens." An enthusiastic sponsor of democracy, the arts, and philosophy, Pericles would dominate the city's politics for over thirty years, fostering a golden age and cementing the city's status as the center of the Greek world, as well as providing the leadership that would write a lasting Athenian legacy in stone above the city.

Pericles' idea was to beautify Athens while providing work for its citizens. It was a plan that would be superbly realized. Appointing the celebrated Athenian sculptor Phidias (c. 480–430 BCE) alongside architects Ictinus (dates unknown) and Callicrates (c. 471–420 BCE) to oversee the project, work began on the cleared and leveled plateau around 447 BCE with the construction of the Parthenon. In fact, it is thought that an older version of the Parthenon was already under construction at the time of the Persian invasion, but whatever remained of that structure was almost completely swept away by the new architects. Instead, they raised a Doric temple with Ionic features, surrounded by a portico of eight columns to each side—in architectural terms, a peripteral octastyle. Such a description, however, fails to capture the Parthenon's exquisite execution. Today, it is considered the greatest architectural and artistic feat of a culture that excelled in these areas.

*Left*: One of Europe's most famous buildings, the ruined Parthenon represents the pinnacle of classical Greek architecture.

*Right*: Located on the southwest slope of the Acropolis, the Odeon of Herodes Atticus was a theater built in 161 CE, and restored in the 1950s. It is still used for performances.

its surrounding columns were carved with a tiny swelling towards the center, which prevented the optical illusion of their having a "waist" when seen from a distance. Standing on a three-stepped platform measuring 69.5 x 30.9 meters (228 x 101 feet), the inner structure itself (known as a *cella*), was 29.8 meters long x 19.2 meters wide (97.8 × 63 feet) and surrounded by forty-six columns. A double row of columns at either end support triangular gables that once contained the fabulous statuary now controversially held by the British Museum in London. Usually described as a temple, it is thought that alongside this function the Parthenon also served as a treasury and meeting area for the confederacy of Greek city states known as the Delian League. The cella also once contained the statue of Athena Parthenos (Athena the Virgin). Completed by Phidias himself—and considered his greatest work at the time—this statue stood about 11.5 meters (37 feet 8 inches) tall.

*Right*: These marble friezes were removed from the Parthenon by the Earl of Elgin in the early nineteenth century and are now in the British Museum, London.

*Below*: A panorama of the Acropolis with the Parthenon to the right and the Propylaea to the left.

Phidias used ivory and about 1,100 kilograms (2,400 pounds) of gold in its construction. Wearing a helmet depicting the Sphinx, raising a spear in one hand while holding a statue of Victory in the other, Athena had a magnificent shield at her feet, the golden reflection of which could be seen by ships miles away. Her gold was stripped in 296 BCE, and replaced with bronze. Later damaged, the statue was looted by the Romans around the fifth century CE and shipped to Constantinople. The last account of it dates to the tenth century.

Elsewhere, the buildings that comprise the Acropolis were equally impressive. The monumental western gate (*propylaea* in Greek), attributed to the architect Mnesicles (dates unknown), provided a suitably awe-inspiring doorway to the complex. Begun around 437 BCE and approached (only by decent citizens who had been ritually washed) by a grand staircase, the entrance echoed the design of the Parthenon with its six Doric columns supporting a similar triangular gable. On either side stood colonnades that featured famous battle scenes and which may have been used for important city events and feasts. The site also boasts numerous other temples, notably the Erechtheion (also attributed to Mnesicles) and dedicated to Athena and Poseidon. Here, visitors find the famous Porch of the Caryatids—the six female statues used as supporting columns. The southwest corner of the Acropolis—to the right of the propylaea entrance—features the Temple of Athena Nike (*nike* means victory), a smaller shrine that could be accessed by any visitor, unlike the rest of the site.

Now sadly bare of the great statues that would once have ornamented its grounds, the Acropolis still dominates the skyline of Athens nearly two and a half thousand years after its construction. Often neglected over the course of the centuries (the Parthenon was partially destroyed by an explosion in 1687 during the Great Turkish War), visitors still find a connection with Greece's ancient beauty and breathtaking invention among its ruins. Now a UNESCO World Heritage Site, and meticulously preserved for future generations, the Acropolis has become an enduring symbol for the sophistication of Ancient Greek civilization, its art, and philosophy. Often referred to as the pinnacle of architectural perfection, its superbly balanced attributes have influenced designers throughout history and can be seen reflected, but never equaled, in monumental buildings around the globe.

*Above right*: Detail of the Erechtheion, showing four of the six maidens that support the Porch of the Caryatids.

*Left*: Standing at the foot of the Acropolis, the Theater of Dionysus could seat up to 17,000 spectators.

| Site information: | |
|---|---|
| **Location:** | Athens, Greece |
| **Type of structure:** | Religious and cultural complex |
| **Area:** | 30,400 square meters (327,220 square feet) |
| **Constructed:** | c. 447–c. 400 BCE |
| **Date of Inscription as a UNESCO World Heritage Site:** | 1987 |
| **UNESCO Criteria:** | (i) (ii) (iii) (iv) (vi) |

# DELPHI
## GREECE

*In ancient Greek myth, Delphi was claimed to be the "navel of the world," and sacred to the god Apollo, who is said to have slain the older dragon-god Python to claim the site.*

THERE ARE OTHER SITES AROUND THE GLOBE WHICH ALSO CLAIM THIS DISTINCTION, including Easter Island, Karnak in Egypt, and the Inca city of Cuzco in Peru. This leads some writers to suggest that the sites may have been connected in the distant past. Delphi was a place of utmost spiritual importance to the Ancient Mediterranean world: a place where the Earth literally touched the realm of the gods. Pilgrims (including Alexander the Great) flocked here from all corners of the Hellenic world—and from as far away as Persia and Egypt—to visit the oracular priestess known as Pythia. Sitting on a tripod over a fissure in the Earth, she inhaled fumes that rose from the depths below. Under their influence she is said to have spoken an unintelligible language—the words of Apollo himself. These were then "translated" by her priests into enigmatic predictions for the future. Located on the slopes of Mount Parnassus in a spectacular position overlooking the Pleistos Valley, the remaining monuments of Delphi occupy a number of terraces and center on the Sanctuary of Apollo, where Pythia once received supplicants. In fact, it is thought that an older Mycenaean oracular cult, possibly dating back to 1700 BCE, may have been present at the site, though it was rededicated to Apollo around 800 BCE. Far from being a simple place of worship, however, as its fame spread Delphi evolved into a small but thriving metropolis, eventually boasting a theater that offered stunning views of the site and the valley below, as well as treasuries that held the rich tributes to Apollo and his oracle (the priests charged for the Pythia's services). In addition, Delphi featured altars, a gymnasium, a stadium that could seat 6,500 spectators—the Pythian games were held here every four years—statues of famous athletes, and smaller shrines and altars.

At the height of Delphi's fame, these buildings would have been sumptuously endowed, as visitors from near and far lavished their wealth to ensure the benevolence of Apollo. However, Delphi was sacked by the Roman general Lucius Cornelius Sulla in 86 BCE, and again on the orders of Emperor Nero in 66 CE. Although attempts were later made to restore the site and maintain its heritage, the rise of Christianity meant that Delphi's glory days were in the past. Emperor Theodosius ordered all pagan sites closed in 393 CE and although Delphi became a Christian sanctuary for a short while, it was abandoned around the seventh century CE.

*Below left*: The Sanctuary of Athena Pronaia at Delphi. The circular building at the center is known as the *tholos*.

*Below*: The Treasury of the Athenians was built to contain donations made to the oracle by the citizens of Athens.

*Right*: Delphi's theater offered its patrons spectacular views over the Pleistos Valley as well as of the action on stage.

Site information:

| | |
|---|---|
| **Location:** | Phocis, Greece |
| **Type of structure:** | Ancient monument, including temples, shrines, theater, and stadium |
| **Area:** | 0.51 square kilometers (0.19 square miles) |
| **Constructed:** | c. 800 BCE–c. 100 BCE |
| **Date of Inscription as a UNESCO World Heritage Site:** | 1987 |
| **UNESCO Criteria:** | (i) (ii) (iii) (iv) (vi) |

# CARNAC STONES
## FRANCE

*In Brittany, close to the village of Carnac, is a collection of over 3,000 standing stones placed in exact linear formations, together with dolmens (single-chamber tombs) and tumuli (earth or stone mounds standing over tombs).*

TO PUT CARNAC INTO CONTEXT, BRITAIN'S MORE FAMOUS STONEHENGE IS THOUGHT TO HAVE ORIGINALLY comprised around just 165 stones (today there are ninety-three). Commonly believed to have served some ritual purpose or to be a large mausoleum complex or to have been erected as a primitive attempt to mark the calendar, Carnac is the largest group of megaliths in the world. No one knows for certain who raised the stones or why. Nevertheless, recent research has revealed possibilities about the site that may make ideas of human history obsolete.

Carnac is, without doubt, a megalithic development on a truly monumental scale. It is correspondingly ancient. Carbon-dating tests put the age of some tombs at a staggering 8,000 years old, while the stones themselves were thought to have been placed in their complex rows around 4500 BCE (more than a thousand years before the stones of Stonehenge were raised). Today, the site bears the inevitable scars

*Left*: The enigmatic stones of Carnac. No one knows for certain why they were arranged in long rows and egg-shaped circles.

of its passage through the millennia. Over the centuries it has been neglected and looted for building materials, while roads have even been built through the arrangements. Even so, it is still possible to discern their original layout.

Some researchers have suggested that there may originally have been up to 10,000 stones at Carnac. Unlike those of Stonehenge these were quarried on site and did not have to be dragged for miles, but the largest remaining stone weighs about 350 tons and still represents a phenomenal engineering achievement for whoever erected it in place. Even the standard stones weigh up to seventy-seven tons. Surrounded by burial sites—the largest of which is known as the tumulus of Saint-Michel and measures 125 x 60 meters (410 x 197 feet)—the stones are laid out in what are commonly seen as four distinct arrangements or "alignments" as they are known. The most westerly is known as the Ménec alignment. Covering an area of 1,165 x 100 meters (3,822 x 328 feet) its eleven rows of stones measure up to 4 meters (13 feet) high at the western end and converge slightly as they proceed to the east. There are 1,100 stones in total. They become smaller towards the center of each line then rise again as they march towards the eastern extremity. At each end are configurations that were probably egg-shaped stone circles when first erected.

To the east is the Kermario alignment, which comprises ten rows (again converging as they progress east) of roughly 1,300 meters (4,300 feet) in length. Its 1,029 stones decrease in size towards the eastern end where the remnants of another circle lie. Yet further east lie the 555 stones of the Kerlescan alignment, which has a similar arrangement: thirteen converging lines of stones that decrease in size from west to east with an overall length of 800 meters (2,600 feet) and a stone circle at the western end. The Kerlescan alignment is thought to be connected to the final alignment (they are now separated by a road), which is known as the Petit-Ménec, and which is hidden in modern woodland. This alignment was heavily mined for stone during the building of a nearby lighthouse, and once comprised three curved lines, stretching about 300 meters (900 feet).

*Above:* One of the hundreds of burial mounds that surround the Carnac Stones. The area seems to have had enormous spiritual significance.

*Right:* The site also has numerous dolmens: burial chambers which were probably once covered in earth and smaller rocks to form a tumulus.

*Below:* Though it may once have contained considerably more stones, the Ménec alignment has—like the rest of the site—suffered from the passage of time. Yet it still boasts an astonishing 1,100 stones of various sizes.

Why did an ancient Neolithic people go to such lengths to build these "stone cathedrals"? Here is a question that has been asked again and again. The legends of centuries past told that the stones were Roman soldiers petrified by the Arthurian wizard Merlin. From the eighteenth century onward, however, the site has been investigated by researchers and archaeologists, giving rise to numerous competing theories. Earlier historians attributed them to the druids, suggesting that the stones might be the remains of prehistoric ritual sites, marking out processional routes lined up to follow the sunrise during equinoxes and leading to sacred spaces or important tombs. Later researchers have proposed the idea of the stones as "star maps" or astronomical observatories (many of the stones mark the moon's orbit). Others have suggested that elements of both theories might be correct and the stones may have been connected to early ideas of both astronomy and religion. It seems likely that, as in other places and times around the globe, science and spirituality were much more entwined than in the present era.

More recently, however, a researcher named Howard Crowhurst—building on the work of Professor Alexander Thom in the 1970s—has identified a sophisticated system of geometry and mathematics bound up in the arrangements of the stones; geometry that is surprisingly comparable to that found in the dimensions of the Great Pyramid as well as other great monuments around the world. As Crowhurst's 1912 book, *Carnac: the Alignments*, demonstrates, the folk who planned and raised Carnac, far from being simple people marking the agricultural year, were working on mathematical principles that are commonly thought to have been discovered by Pythagoras. This idea that our most distant ancestors were playing with complex mathematics surfaces time and again during research into the most ancient monuments and raises fascinating questions for today's students of prehistory: if Crowhurst and others are correct, then how did these supposedly "primitive" people acquire such knowledge and what were they using it for?

Research such as Crowhurst's might give us a glimpse of a distant age but it remains hard to know why these stones were arranged as they are. Whoever put them in place left behind no writing and precious few artifacts through which we can attempt to discern their history or culture. Because they lived at such an impossibly distant time, we imagine that the builders represent humanity at its most crude. But we may well be wrong. Carnac, and other sites around the world, seem to hold out the tantalizing suggestion that even our most distant ancestors were far more sophisticated than we commonly credit.

*Left*: One of three dolmens in a group known as the Dolmens of Mané-Kerioned, this structure features a corridor that would have led into the burial chamber.

**Site information:**

| | |
|---|---|
| Location: | Brittany, France |
| Type of structure: | Standing stones; megalithic monuments |
| Area: | c. 0.4 square kilometers (0.15 square miles) |
| Constructed: | c. 4500–c. 3500 BCE |

**Date of Inscription as a UNESCO World Heritage Site:** Submitted by France to the UNESCO "tentative list" in 1996

**UNESCO Criteria:** Cultural (pre-2004 submission)

# PONT DU GARD
## FRANCE

*Built around the mid-first century CE, the Pont du Gard is one of the best-preserved of all surviving Roman aqueducts and a work of brilliant architecture, incorporating an equally impressive engineering genius in its construction.*

PART OF A 50-KILOMETER (31-MILE) WATER SYSTEM, THE SUPERBLY ELEGANT AQUEDUCT HELPED TO CARRY WATER FROM THE FONTAINE D'EURE NEAR UZÈS TO THE ROMAN TOWN OF NEMAUSUS (modern day Nîmes) using only gravity to power the flow. In order to do so, the bridge itself incorporates a tiny gradient of 1:18,241 across its 274-meter (899-foot) length: a drop of just 2.5 centimeters (1 inch) from one end to the other.

The man responsible for the design is commonly held to have been Marcus Vipsanius Agrippa (c. 64 BCE–12 CE), son-in-law to the Emperor Augustus, and a successful general and politician as well as a noted architect whose civic works helped beautify and cleanse the imperial city. He designed numerous public buildings as well as improving Rome's sewer system. Despite this, more recent

archaeological finds put the construction of the aqueduct to between 40 and 60 CE, years after Agrippa's death, so it is possible that the work of an unsung architect has been attributed to him.

Whoever was responsible, the Pont du Gard is a masterpiece. Rising on three levels of arches to a height of just under 49 meters (160 feet) above the Gardon river, it was constructed of an attractive, soft yellow-pink local limestone—known as Pierre de Vers—over a period of approximately fifteen years. Each arch is slightly different in span, helping to guard the bridge against subsidence, while the width of the bridge tapers with each tier from a base of 9 meters (30 feet) to a slender 3.8 meters (9.8 feet) at the top, where the water channel (known as a *specus*) runs. Archaeologists inspecting the bridge have discovered remnants of the original building works, including scaffolding points

and numbered blocks—the latter an indication that the site was meticulously well organized.

When first built, the aqueduct helped carry around 200,000 cubic meters (44,000,000 gallons) of water each day to Nîmes, filling the baths and fountains, and quenching the thirst of the citizens. Today, it is no longer in use but is a popular tourist attraction and beauty spot that stands as a testament to the engineering and architectural know-how of the Roman Empire.

*Above*: Built of a local stone called Pierre de Vers, the Pont du Gard's scaffolding points and other features of the aqueduct's construction can still be seen in situ.

*Opposite page*: A panoramic view of the aqueduct's entire span with the Gardon river below.

### Site information:

| | |
|---|---|
| Location: | Gard, France |
| Type of structure: | Stone-built aqueduct bridge |
| Length: | 274 meters (899 feet) |
| Height: | 48.8 meters (160 feet) |
| Constructed: | c. 40–60 CE |
| Date of Inscription as a UNESCO World Heritage Site: | 2007 |
| UNESCO Criteria: | (i) (iii) (iv) |

# LASCAUX
## FRANCE

*Twenty thousand years ago, the world was in the grip of an ice age that pushed vast glaciers over northern Europe. Further south, however, human beings had established a foothold.*

LIFE MUST HAVE BEEN HARD WHEN THE HEIGHT OF MODERN TECHNOLOGY WAS THE NEEDLE AND THREAD. Every tool was made of bone, horn, or stone—all of which were laboriously worked by hand. Food was either hunted or gathered from the wild, a time-consuming and often dangerous necessity that must have frequently left these Stone Age people hungry. Yet despite these constraints, the people of the Upper Paleolithic age developed astonishing artistic skill, using complex compounds and simple tools to create images that strike the art critics of today as being as confident and powerful as those of any modern artist. The most famous of their monuments is to be found in the Dordogne department of southwest France. In the caves of Lascaux are almost 2,000 images— abstract designs, animals, and human figures as well as depictions of constellations—that are globally recognized as the greatest collection of Stone Age artwork yet discovered.

The caves were found in September, 1940, by a young man named Marcel Ravidat, and were opened to the public in 1948. At that time the entrance was covered by a simple shed and visitors had to wriggle through a tight entrance into the caves on their bottoms. Even so, as the caves' fame spread, up to 1,200 visitors per day arrived to witness the prehistoric marvels daubed onto the walls. Lascaux attracted so many visitors, in fact, that by the 1960s the carbon dioxide, airborne contaminants, and body heat generated by such a large number of human bodies had visibly taken its toll on the artwork. In 1963 the caves were closed and the paintings restored. Today, the originals are closely monitored while visitors are invited to see reproductions of the paintings in a recreation of the caves that is, in itself, hugely impressive. Created over eleven years, more than twenty artists worked on the replica using the materials and techniques of the ancient artists to achieve an authentic copy.

As Ravidat discovered, the original caves are a network of passageways and "rooms" liberally covered with ancient artworks in ochres, reds, yellows, and blacks—the colors obtained by mixing pounded minerals with water, clay, or animal fat. Only the simplest of tools was used in their execution. The artists possessed no brushes, though a primitive air-brush effect was obtained by blowing paint through tubes. Closest to the entrance is a chamber known as the Hall of the Bulls. Here, bulls and aurochs (a now extinct species of cattle) run alongside horses and deer. The largest painting is the biggest single representation of an animal ever discovered in Paleolithic art, measuring 5.2 meters (17 feet) long.

Two passages lead away from the head of the Hall of the Bulls. To the southeast runs the relatively short—22-meter (72-foot) Axial Gallery, which many art experts agree contain the finest works in

the cave system. Here a host of animals swirl in seeming confusion, including the famous Great Black Bull (which was executed using the spray paint method), as well as ibexes, horses, cows, and aurochs. Displaying fantastic skill, the painters used the natural planes of the cave walls to develop perspectives and—as elsewhere—superbly captured the movement and vitality of their subjects.

A longer passage heads south from the Hall of Bulls, containing distinct "galleries" known as The Passageway, the Nave, the Mondmilch Gallery (which is unadorned due to the crumbly texture of its surfaces), and the Chamber of the Feline, which—unusually—contains depictions of felines, including mating lions. About a quarter of the way down,

a passage running to the west leads to the Shaft: a hole in the ground where the rare depiction of a human can be found fighting a bison, as well as a small cavern with a diameter of c. 4.5 meters (15 feet). Known as the Apse, it is thought that this space may have been an important ceremonial site. It is richly endowed with animal paintings as well as abstract designs and notable images such as the Great Sorcerer.

Why these caves contain such a rich profusion of art is a question that has fascinated archaeologists since their discovery. Based on the fact that no natural features such as trees or rivers were ever depicted, as well as other artifacts found in the caves, it seems likely that they were used for some type of spiritual ceremonies connected to hunting.

*Previous page, left*: Detail from the ceiling of the Hall of the Bulls, where bulls run with horses, deer, and the now-extinct aurochs.

*Previous page, right*: Despite their primitive tools, the ancient artists at Lascaux painted images of delicacy and power.

*Opposite page*: The caves contain a total of almost 2,000 paintings. On seeing them for the first time Picasso is said to have declared, "We have created nothing new."

*Below left*: The modern entrance to the caves is a vast improvement on the days when visitors shuffled in on their bottoms.

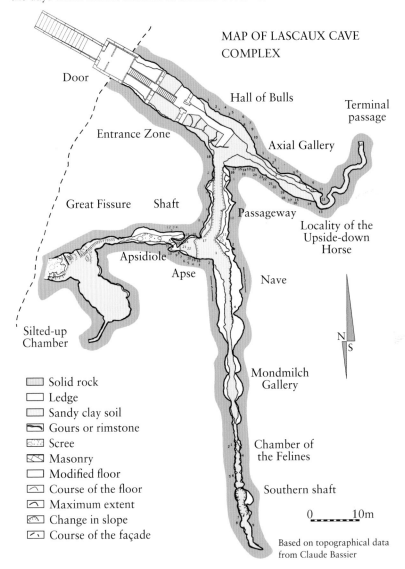

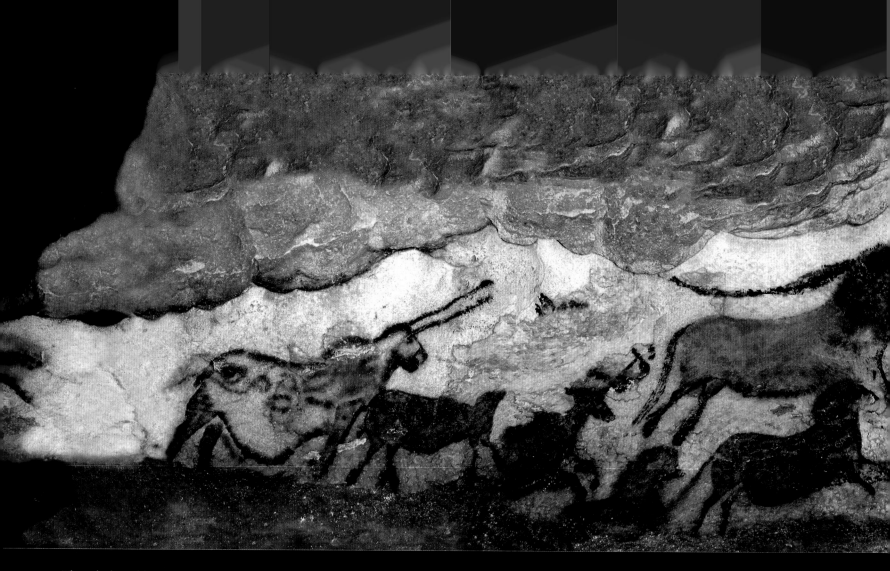

The scholar Abbe Henri Breuil, a leading expert in prehistoric art, has suggested that the paintings comprise a "magical" ritual designed to control the animals' behavior. Others, however, point to the fact that the footprints of numerous adolescents were discovered at the site. They wonder if the Lascaux caves might have been used for ritual initiations when a member of the tribe reached adulthood.

Whatever their purpose, the caves are a singular connection to a human history that has been almost entirely clouded by the mists of millennia. And once again we are reminded that even in the most distant reaches of the past, humans displayed sophisticated skills. Our ancestors may not have discovered the wheel, but they possessed an artistic virtuosity that continues to amaze us after 20,000 years.

*Top*: Known as the Panel of the Unicorn this artwork appears in the Nave area and is a superb expression of the artists' skill.

*Above*: Visitors in the early 1960s. Today's tourists are invited to view a replica of the caves to avoid further damage to the original artworks.

Poiters

Paris

Lascaux

*FRANCE*

Limoges

Angoulême

*Puy de Sancy* ▲

*MASSIF*

**Lascaux**

*Mont du Luguet* ▲

Brive-la-Gaillarde

*Puy Mary* ▲

Bergerac

*CENTRAL*

*Dordogne*

Cahors

### Site information:

| | |
|---|---|
| **Location:** | Dordogne, France |
| **Type of structure:** | Cave system containing Paleolithic artwork |
| **Area:** | Combined length of cave complex is c. 200 meters (650 feet) |
| **Constructed:** | c. 17,000 BCE |
| **Date of Inscription as a UNESCO World Heritage Site:** | 1979 |
| **UNESCO Criteria:** | (i) (iii) |

# ARLES
## FRANCE

*Beloved by emperors, as well as by artists including Vincent Van Gogh (who left around 300 artworks depicting the city and its surroundings), the city of Arles in southern France is one of the most stunningly beautiful cities in a country that has far more than its fair share of picturesque towns.*

SITUATED AT THE MOUTH OF THE RHÔNE RIVER, AND RENOWNED AS A GATEWAY TO THE MAGNIFICENT LANDSCAPE OF THE CAMARGUE WETLANDS, Arles also possesses a history that stretches back almost 3,000 years. It is, however, the beautifully preserved buildings and relics dating to the Roman era that have cemented the citys reputation as a site of outstanding cultural and historical significance.

Named Arelate, the city became a Roman possession in 123 BCE, and thanks to the addition of a canal (built in 104 BCE) that connected it to the Mediterranean, quickly assumed a new importance as a trading port, though in direct competition with Massalia (modern Marseilles) further along the coast. However, when Massalia supported Pompey during the civil war that would eventually see Julius Caesar (100–44 BCE) become the Roman dictator and de facto emperor in 48 BCE its fate was sealed. Instead, further eastwards, Arelate had helped to bolster Caesar's force and was rewarded with its rival's territories, assuming the position of preeminent port on the coast of Gaul. Fully Romanized, Arelate swiftly became a cultural and religious hub over the following centuries as well as an important base for military campaigns into Gaul as well as for the Christian church as it pushed its message northward.

A favorite city of emperor Constantine I (272–337 CE) its influence gradually declined as the Roman Empire crumbled, though its Roman patrons bequeathed it a superb architectural legacy.

Principal among Arles' many fine Roman structures is the largely intact, two-tiered amphitheater at the heart of the city. Built in 90 CE to hold a capacity crowd of 20,000 spectators for gladiator battles and chariot races, it is a spectacular example of its type, measuring 136 meters (446 feet) in length and 109 meters (358 feet) in width. Drawing inspiration from the Colosseum in Rome, its exterior features two levels of elegant arches. While no longer providing gladiators, the amphitheater's ancient traditions can still be seen in the bullfights it regularly hosts today.

Also well preserved—though not fully excavated—are the Baths of Constantine, which were built as part of the emperor's palace during the fourth century CE. Constructed in characteristic Romanesque style (which incorporated the use of long, flat brickwork and simple, graceful

forms) the baths today offer a fascinating glimpse of life into the upper echelons of Roman society. The hypocaust (which provided underfloor heating), warm air room, and caldarium (warm bath) are still visible.

Elsewhere, flavors of Arles' imperial past can be seen in its lovely forum, the remnants of which stand in an area that is home to cafés. As it would have done when constructed in the first century CE, the Roman social and political center still buzzes with life. Beneath the Place du Forum underground galleries constructed at the same time can still be visited through an entrance in the town hall.

Outside the ancient city walls lies the Alyscamps burial site, which lay along the Roman Aurelian Way and served as the city's main necropolis for around 1,500 years. Roman law forbade burials within the city and the swelling population of Arles meant that this fabulous

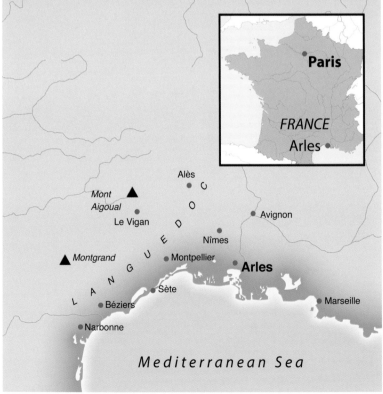

*Previous page, left:* The Alyscamps necropolis dates back to Roman times and was one of the most fashionable burial sites in Europe.

*Previous page, right:* The Arles amphitheater was built in 90 CE and seated up to 20,000 Roman spectators for spectacles of gladiatorial combat. It is still in use almost 2,000 years later.

*Opposite page:* A detail showing hunters using nets, from a Roman-period sarcophagus found in the Alyscamps necropolis.

*Above:* As well as a large amphitheater, Arles also boasts a smaller theater where audiences would have watched dramatic productions.

### Site information:

| | |
|---|---|
| **Location:** | Bouches-du-Rhône, France |
| **Type of structure:** | Numerous significant Roman buildings |
| **Area:** | 0.65 square kilometers (0.25 square miles) |
| **Constructed:** | First to fourth centuries CE |
| **Date of Inscription as a UNESCO World Heritage Site:** | 1981 |
| **UNESCO Criteria:** | (ii) (iv) |

graveyard grew alongside the city. Wealthy inhabitants vied with one another to build grand and tasteful mausoleums for family members and the result was already recognized as one of the most prestigious resting sites in Roman times. So exulted, in fact, that bodies from across Europe were brought here to be interred in its fashionable surroundings. Although the necropolis later suffered from looting (city officials during the Renaissance period are said to have given away important Roman relics as gifts), Alyscamps retains much of the serene beauty that lured Vincent van Gogh and his friend Paul Gauguin to paint among its tombs and sarcophagi.

Further afield, Arles boasts an aqueduct and a Roman mill that explain how the ancient civilization produced sufficient food to satisfy the flourishing town on an industrial scale. An engineering marvel, it would once have milled around 4.5 tons of flour each day. Together, such remnants of the Roman world provide a fascinating physical record of European life during Roman times and remain a testament to the empire's might, architectural prowess, and refinement.

*Right:* The remains of the Roman aqueduct which brought water to Arles from the small mountain range called the Alpilles.

*Below:* Subterranean galleries under the Roman forum may once have served as slave pens.

# VALLEY OF THE TEMPLES, AGRIGENTO
## SICILY

Magna Graecia—*meaning Great Greece*—was the name given to the spread of Greek peoples and their culture across the *Mediterranean world before the rise of the Roman Empire.*

*Right:* This statue of Atlas is one of a number that once helped to hold up the roof of the Temple of Olympian Zeus. Each statue was 7.5 metres (25 feet) tall.

*Below left:* The Temple of Concordia is one of the best-preserved examples of Greek temple building in the world.

*Below:* The circular altar can be found in the Sanctuary of Chthonic Gods (the gods of the underworld).

LEAVING A LASTING IMPRESSION ON THEIR SUCCESSORS, THE REMAINS OF GREEK COLONIES CAN BE FOUND FROM THE BLACK SEA TO LIBYA. It was, however, at Agrigento in Sicily that settlers built their finest city—a metropolis that rivaled any in Greece itself. Known to its people as Akragas and eventually supporting an estimated population of up to 200,000, the city was founded c. 582 BCE and became one of the most important ports of the Hellenic world.

Its citizens left behind a stunning architectural legacy; a masterpiece of urban planning, Akragas boasted defensive walls, a beautiful agora (the center of public life), subterranean aqueducts, and—set on craggy ridges above the valley, dominating the spectacular landscape—eight magnificent temples.

Perhaps the best-known is the Temple of Concordia, which provided inspiration for the UNESCO logo. Arguably the best-preserved Greek temple in the world, it was built in an area where a level of clay

lies beneath the rock surface. Crucially, this natural shock absorber protected the building during earthquakes. Resembling the Parthenon in design but built on a smaller scale, this measures 39.4 x 16.9 meters (129 × 55 feet) at the base of the four steps that lead up to the temple. While the roof has long since gone, much of the structure, including its thirty-eight Doric columns, remain intact.

The fact that the Temple of Concordia was converted to Christian use in the sixth century CE also helped ensure its survival. The seven other temples built on the ridge—to Hera, Heracles, Olympian Zeus, Castor and Pollux, Hephaestus, Demeter, and Asclepius—have not been so lucky. Shaken by earthquakes and looted for building materials, none has stood the passage of the centuries as well. Even so, among the ruins are glimpses of life in ancient Akragas. Beyond the colonnade of the Temple of Hera, for example, is a sacrificial altar.

As much of the old city remains unexcavated, Akragas may still have a lot to teach us. Nevertheless, what remains visible today is a superb expression of a culture that has made a significant impact on the development of Western culture.

*Above:* The ruins of the Temple of Heracles. As its name suggests, the temple was dedicated to the mythical hero and once contained a large statue of him.

*Opposite page:* The reassembled remains of the Temples of Castor and Pollux, twin brothers from Ancient Greek mythology.

### Site information:

| | |
|---|---|
| **Location:** | Agrigento, Sicily |
| **Type of structure:** | Greek temples |
| **Area:** | 9.34 square kilometers (3.6 square miles) |
| **Constructed:** | c. 500–420 BCE |
| **Date of Inscription as a UNESCO World Heritage Site:** | 1997 |
| **UNESCO Criteria:** | (i) (ii) (iii) (iv) |

# THE COLOSSEUM
## ROME, ITALY

*Known as the Flavian Amphitheater for the first thousand years of its existence, Rome's famous Colosseum is thought to have taken its current name from the colossal statue of Emperor Nero that once stood nearby (the base can still be seen today).*

THE LARGEST AMPHITHEATER EVER BUILT BY THE ROMANS, THE COLOSSEUM WAS ABLE TO SEAT UP TO 80,000 SPECTATORS AT ITS SPECTACLES and is considered one of the great architectural feats of the Roman Empire. Completed in 80 CE, the Colosseum was begun on the orders of the Flavian Emperor Vespasian (9–79 CE) in 72 CE following the death of the hated Nero (37–68 CE) and subsequent four-year war over the imperial succession. The former emperor was widely despised and Vespasian began his own rule with a popular gesture—seizing Nero's private pleasure grounds (which he had appropriated after the Great Fire of Rome in 64 CE) and returning them to public use with an amphitheater as the focal point. Completed under the rule of his heir, Titus (39–81 CE), the building that Vespasian ordered built proved an architectural triumph.

Measuring 189 x 156 meters (615 x 510 feet), the Colosseum is a vast oval covering an area of 24,000 square meters (more than 250,000 square feet) and rising above the streets of Rome in a series of three layers of arches, separated by carved half-columns and topped with a windowed level. Around the top, builders added 240 corbels that once would have anchored the vast awning that protected spectators from the rain and sun. Within is the arena itself—87 meters (287 feet) long by 55 meters (180 feet) wide—and surrounded by tiers of seating separated from the arena by a wall. At each end were private boxes used by the emperor himself and the Vestal Virgins. Beneath the arena lies a double-level complex of tunnels and cells that were used to contain combatants and wild animals as well as for raising scenery into position during the spectacular entertainments hosted here.

Those ancient spectacles were extraordinarily grisly. The Colosseum's blood-soaked arena was once the site of gladiatorial battles, mass executions, and elaborately staged battles. Contemporary reports state that 9,000 animals—including crocodiles, rhinos, and elephants as well as lions, tigers, panthers, and bears—were killed during the stadium's inaugural games alone. The number of human deaths was comparatively huge and included the execution of criminals during intervals between the main events. One estimate suggests that up to 400,000 people lost their lives in the Colosseum's arena over the four centuries it was in use for public shows—although the number of deaths would have been far higher during the earlier centuries before the rise of Christianity gradually changed the nature of the "games." The last gladiatorial fight took place in the early fifth century, though large numbers of animal continued to be killed during staged "hunts" for at least another century.

Despite having been damaged by war and earthquakes, and looted for its travertine stone over the centuries, the Colosseum remains a symbol of an empire that was as cruel and brutal as it was powerful and refined. Its glorious architecture and bloody history represent both the heights and depths of the human spirit.

*Above right:* A bird's eye view of the Colosseum gives an idea of the amphitheater's sheer size. In its heyday it would have been packed with noisy crowds of up to 80,000 people including the emperor himself and the Vestal Virgins.

*Left:* Once the site of horrific bloodshed, the Colosseum is now lit up in golden lights whenever a death sentence is commuted somewhere in the world.

**Site information:**

| | |
|---|---|
| **Location:** | Rome, Italy |
| **Type of structure:** | Amphitheater |
| **Length:** | 189 meters (615 feet) |
| **Width:** | 156 meters (510 feet) |
| **Height:** | 48 meters (157 feet) |
| **Constructed:** | c. 72–80 CE |

**Date of Inscription as a UNESCO World Heritage Site:** 1980

**UNESCO Criteria:** (i) (ii) (iii) (iv) (vi)

# THE FORUM
## ROME, ITALY

*At its height, the Roman Empire sprawled across the known world—from Britain in the north to Egypt in the south; from the Atlantic shores of Spain to ancient Babylonia in the east.*

AT THE HEART OF THIS VAST EMPIRE LAY ITS CAPITAL CITY, AND AT THE HEART OF ROME LAY THE FORUM. Clustered around its central square stood statues of the great and triumphal arches, palaces and shrines, taverns and shops, as well as the Senate House and offices for the empire's administrators. Its precincts witnessed the triumphs of returning generals, the speeches of great orators such as Cicero (106–43 BCE), elections, criminal trials, and gladiatorial combat—the seething life of a vast and powerful empire.

All this activity took place in and around an area measuring approximately 250 x 170 meters (820 x 560 feet) not far from the Colosseum at the end of the Via Sacra (Sacred Way). In use from the earliest days of Rome in the seventh century BCE, the Forum lies in the valley between the feet of the Palatine and Capitoline hills and saw almost constant construction work as the empire grew and ever grander buildings were raised to reflect Roman might (later archaeologists would find numerous layers of building works beneath the level of the current Forum). Eventually, the mass of buildings reduced the size of the rectangular open courtyard at the Forum's center to 130 x 50 meters (425 x 165 feet).

A full account of the many historically important buildings here would require a book in itself, but notable structures include the Curia Julia—built by Julius Caesar in 44 BCE as a meeting place for the Senate—and the white marble arch of Septimus Severus (203 CE), which celebrated victories over the Parthians. In front of the Curia, a piece of black marble—the Lapis Niger—marks the supposed site of the grave of Romulus, the fabled founder of Rome. To the left of the triumphal arch are the remaining columns of the Temple of Saturn, which was built in 283 CE on the site of earlier temples. Elsewhere, can

be seen the three remaining columns of the Temple of Castor and Pollux. Previously the Senate's meeting place, the temple dates back to 485 BCE and also served as an early Roman banking area for money changers—as well as barbers—all clustering on its steps. Also still visible are the ruins of the Regia (the palace of Roman kings before the Republic was established) as well as the Temple of Vesta and the House of the Vestal Virgins. Here, the priestesses of Vesta once carried out their sacred rites in seclusion within the beautiful surrounds of their palace and sacred grove.

Today, the Forum lies in ruins, its once mighty buildings reduced by centuries of neglect and stripped of their stone to provide building materials for later structures. Since the eighteenth century, however, the Forum's significance as the ancient hub of the Roman Empire has become widely recognized and it is now well protected.

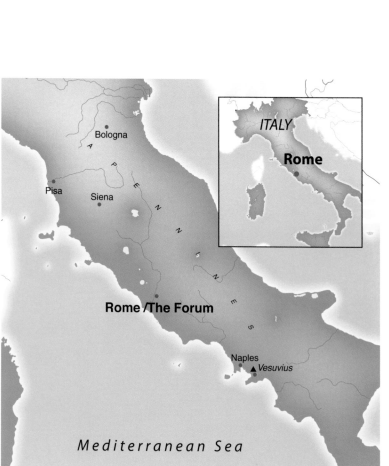

*Above:* The ruins of the circular Temple of Vesta, which once stood in the sanctuary's sacred grove.

*Opposite page:* A view over the Forum. The columned portico in the center belonged to the Temple of Saturn, the monument directly behind it is the Arch of Septimus Severus.

| Site information: | |
|---|---|
| **Location:** | Rome, Italy |
| **Type of structure:** | Various buildings comprising the ancient city center |
| **Area:** | 42,500 square meters (257,500 square feet) |
| **Constructed:** | c. eighth century BCE to fourth century CE |
| **Date of Inscription as a UNESCO World Heritage Site:** 1980 | |
| **UNESCO Criteria:** | (i) (ii) (iii) (iv) (vi) |

# POMPEII
## ITALY

*At some time between August 24 and November 23 (contemporary documents and archaeological evidence give conflicting dates), in the year 79 CE, Mount Vesuvius erupted with a thermal ferocity estimated to have been 100,000 times greater than that released by the atom bombs of World War II.*

THE NEARBY TOWNS OF HERCULANEUM AND POMPEII WERE FIRST SEARED BY INTENSE HEAT EXCEEDING 250°C (482°F), then inundated by falling rock and ash that had been blasted up to 33 kilometers (21 miles) into the atmosphere. Across the bay, in Naples, the celebrated Roman writer Pliny the Younger (61–c. 113 CE) watched in horror as his uncle, Pliny the Elder, rallied ships of the Roman navy in a rescue attempt that would cost him his life. Within hours the town was buried beneath a thick layer of volcanic debris. Life in the bustling Roman town had come to an abrupt and permanent stop.

As the centuries passed, Pompeii, Herculaneum, and the smaller settlements around them were completely forgotten until builders constructing a waterway in 1599 unearthed a wall covered with Roman artwork. The architect Domenico Fontana (1543–1607) excavated further, but—alarmed by the erotic nature of the frescoes he discovered—covered them up again. Again, Pompeii was forgotten. In 1738, however, workers building a palace for Charles of Bourbon (1716–1788), the King of Naples, unearthed a part of Herculaneum. Intrigued, Charles ordered more digging. Pompeii was discovered in

1748. Finding it much easier to excavate than Herculaneum (Pompeii's layer of ash was considerably thinner) his workers and successive archaeological teams uncovered ever more of the ancient town.

The excavation of the site represents one of the greatest archaeological events in history. Elsewhere—as we have already seen in this book—the past has been defaced by the passage of centuries: buildings robbed of their contents, vandalized for their stone, and broken by earthquakes and human conflict. In Pompeii, however, ash falling onto the town later solidified, preserving beneath the new ground level a successful town as it had been at the moment of the eruption. Artwork, jewelry, tools, lamps, furniture, and even foodstuffs from every dwelling remained trapped beneath the stone—capturing a perfect snapshot of Roman life, from the villas of the wealthy to the dwellings of slaves.

Even the citizens were caught at the moment of their death. Although their bodies decayed, the spaces they had occupied remained in the rock. By filling these voids with plaster, excavators created touching life size molds in the shapes made by Pompeii's dead.

The amount of data provided by Vesuvius's cataclysmic eruption is incredible. At the time of its sudden burial Pompeii was a successful holiday town and agricultural area with around 10,000 permanent citizens. Close to the Bay of Naples and enjoying a warm climate as well as rich soil, it was a center of entertainment, farming, and viticulture—a microcosm of Roman life. The wealthy built holiday homes here, while the poor shared smaller homes built around patches of land where they raised crops that helped feed their families. The town's paved streets were home to many businesses, including small factories and shops, taverns, restaurants, a hotel, and at least one brothel alongside the other staples of Roman life—baths, temples, theaters, and an imposing 20,000-seat amphitheater.

Although the layout of the city (straight roads conforming to the Roman's obsession with order) is informative, the real fasciation lies in the smaller artifacts found at Pompeii. In these things we find evidence of everyday life that paint vivid details in the bigger picture of Roman life. For example, a giraffe bone found in the drains outside a restaurant suggest that the town's citizens enjoyed an extremely varied diet, while a perfectly preserved loaf of bread shows that bakers stamped their wares. Customers who sent slaves to the shops might have wanted to be sure

*Previous pages:* This panoramic photograph of Pompeii's Forum demonstrates the excellent condition of buildings that lay beneath a layer of thick ash for almost 2,000 years.

*Opposite page:* Pompeii's theater area boasted two theaters—the Odeon and the 5,000-seat Large Theater, pictured here.

*Above:* Religion played an important part in the daily life of Roman citizens. As well as great temples they built smaller shrines where offerings could be left.

*Left:* A bronze statue outside Pompeii's Temple of Apollo.

that they weren't skimming a profit by visiting cheaper bakeries. The town is also rich in graffiti, of which the Romans were big fans. Daubed or scratched on walls are complaints about errant husbands and dining guests, touching declarations of love and friendship, word games, and—of course—many, many vulgarities, some of them earthy but hilarious and including confessions of dalliances, coarse gossip, and the mocking of individuals' sexual performance.

In fact, Pompeii was a thoroughly bawdy place. From the most opulent villas to the commonest parts of town, erotic paintings and sexually charged artifacts were found that later authorities considered too immoral and shocking for public display. These, they either covered up (in the case of frescoes) or locked away far from sight. After more

than two centuries the "Secret Museum" of Naples was only fully opened to the public in 2000.

Where many ancient sites guard their mysteries closely, Pompeii has given us a dazzlingly sharp image of Roman life. In many ways it was little different from our own. Pompeii's citizens went to the theater, prepared meals, visited temples, drank and made merry in taverns, and enjoyed company. Their deaths were sudden and tragic but, at the same time, Vesuvius preserved aspects of their ways that might otherwise have been forgotten: their humor, everyday complaints, sexuality, and so much more. One piece of graffiti puts it simply: "Satura was here."

*Above:* While excavating Pompeii pockets of space containing human remains were found. Filled with plaster (or a special resin these days) they formed touching effigies of the people who died in the Vesuvius's catastrophic eruption.

*Left:* A mosaic of a naked woman and satyr. Artifacts, graffiti, and artworks found in the ancient town suggest that Roman citizens were very comfortable with expressions of sexuality.

*Opposite page:* A vividly decorated room in the House of Gaius Cuspius Pansa. The square hole in the center of the room, the *impluvium*, is a basin that collected rainwater from an opening in the roof.

### Site information:

| | |
|---|---|
| **Location:** | Pompeii, Italy |
| **Type of structure:** | Preserved Roman town |
| **Area:** | 0.65 square kilometers (0.25 square miles) |
| **Constructed:** | c. seventh century BCE–79 CE |
| **Date of Inscription as a UNESCO World Heritage Site:** | 1997 |
| **UNESCO Criteria:** | (iii) (iv) (v) |

# STONEHENGE
## UNITED KINGDOM

*Few ancient monuments are as famous as Stonehenge. Set among a wealth of Neolithic and Bronze Age monuments, including hundreds of burial mounds and earthworks, the site has become a worldwide symbol of ancient mystery, puzzled over by successive generations.*

PHYSICALLY, THE MONUMENT REPRESENTS AN INCREDIBLE FEAT OF NEOLITHIC ENGINEERING, as well as vast age. Located on Salisbury Plain, near Amesbury in Wiltshire, the site is thought to have acquired spiritual or astronomical significance at least 10,000 years ago. Pits in which wooden posts were once set date to this period and run along an east–west axis, suggesting they may have been used as a calendar, measuring out the solstices. The Stonehenge we now see is thought to have been built in stages from 5,000 to 4,000 years ago. Although little is certain, the consensus of opinion is that the megalith known as the Heel Stone and a circular ditch with a diameter of around 98 meters (320 feet) were probably the first to appear. Just inside the earthworks are holes that may once have been the foundations for an earlier, wooden, version of the circle. Around 2500 BCE, however, the ancient builders abandoned wood as a building material. Instead, they began transporting to the site giant sarsen stones from a quarry about 40 kilometers (25 miles) to the north, as well as smaller bluestone rocks from the Preseli Hills in Wales—about 240 kilometers (150 miles) away. With the largest sarsen stones weighing up to 50 tonnes, and measuring up to 9 meters (30 feet), how they did this has always been one of Stonehenge's great mysteries, but in 1995 a 100-strong team demonstrated that a 40-tonne slab of rock could be pulled across a considerable distance on a greased sled. Nevertheless, bringing the stones through dense woodland remains an almost unbelievable achievement.

Why the builders of Stonehenge went to such efforts is also unclear, though a study by London's Royal College of Art found that the Welsh bluestone rocks have sonic properties that make them ring like bells. Professor Tim Darvill—a leading expert on Stonehenge—suggests that the circle may once have been played like "a pre-historic glockenspiel."

*Left:* A view through the outer ring. The site may have been used as a giant calendar with the outer ring used to calculate the full year and the inner horseshoe the lunar month.

*Right:* This aerial photograph clearly shows Stonehenge's outer ring and the horseshoe shape of the inner trilithons.

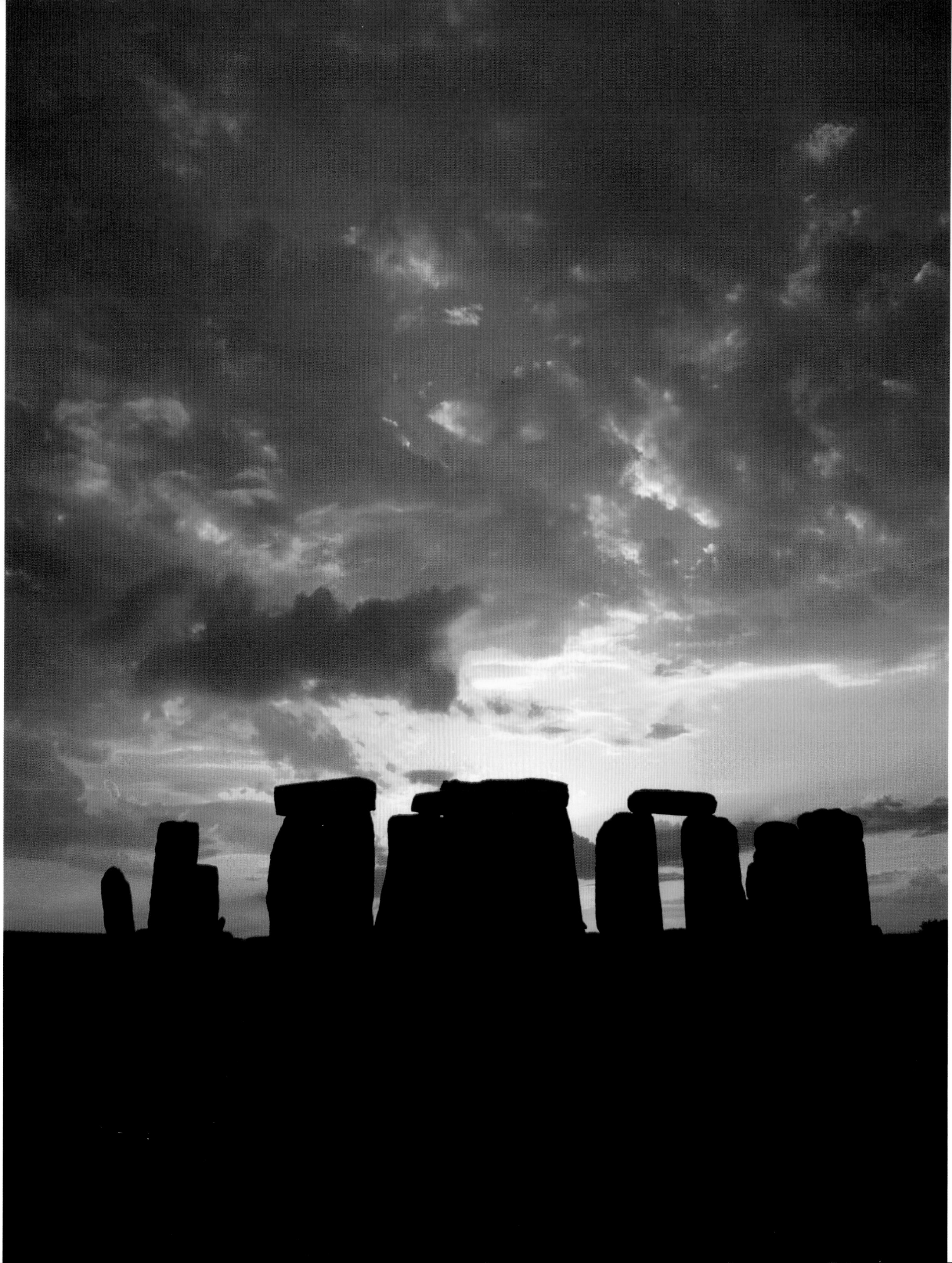

*Left:* Sunsets and sunrises at Stonehenge are enchanting, which has led many modern "druids" to imagine it was a sacred site. Ironically, it is almost certain that Stonehenge was not used by the ancient druids.

*Below:* The first mention of Stonehenge in British literature dates to 1130, at which time it was called "Staneges."

On site, the stones were raised into position, then rearranged (probably over a period of about 300–400 years) into the final configuration: a circle of sarsens capped with lintels (many have now toppled and some of the stones have been removed from the site) enclosing an inner horseshoe of five trilithons (two vertical stones with a lintel), of which three are still standing. Close to the center is the altar stone, now obscured by a fallen trilithon. Further stones marked the entrance to the site with an earthwork "avenue" connecting the site to the River Avon.

Early stories tell that Stonehenge was set in place by Merlin, marking the burial site of Uther Pendragon, King Arthur's father, while other fables credit the Devil with the construction. More recently, archaeologists, scientists, researchers, and armchair theorists have supplied almost ceaseless—and head-spinning—speculations. The fact that Stonehenge was organized to align with the summer and winter solstices has led many researchers to imagine that the circle was once used as an astronomical observatory, though there are a host of other theories. Around Stonehenge are burial sites that contain the bodies of people who had suffered injury or who had other physical defects. Some of these "pilgrims" appear to have traveled from as far afield as the Mediterranean and Germany. Professor Darvill believes this indicates that Stonehenge may have been seen as a healing site, or an ancient Lourdes. The large number of burial sites in the area has also been seen as evidence that Stonehenge was used in ancient rituals for the dead, and possibly for ancestor worship. In his book, *Solving Stonehenge*, landscape archaeologist Anthony Johnson points out that Stonehenge's layout incorporates sophisticated geometry, in much the same way that Howard Crowhurst demonstrated at Carnac. Others

have suggested that the site is aligned with other ancient monuments around Britain and further afield, or was a symbol of peace built at a time when British tribes were coming together. Curiously, one of the most popular theories—that Stonehenge was a site sacred to the druids—has been widely discredited. In fact, the druidic cult is thought to have risen much later in British history and the little we know about it indicates the druids were probably more comfortable performing their rituals in natural sites, such as forest clearings.

Over the years, the ninety-three stones that can still be seen at the site have attracted millions of visitors from across the globe and, today, occupy a unique place in British heritage. Why Stonehenge has fascinated so many is something of a mystery in itself. There are more than a thousand stone circles and megalith sites across Europe, many of which seem far more impressive. Yet something about Stonehenge speaks to us across the millennia in a voice that is impossible to ignore, presenting a riddle that has long confounded the most intelligent minds.

*Above:* Another evocative photograph of the site. Note the small dome on top of the central stone. This would have fitted into a corresponding hole in the lintel to secure it in place.

### Site information:

| | |
|---|---|
| **Location:** | Salisbury Plain, United Kingdom |
| **Type of structure:** | Megalithic circle |
| **Diameter of surrounding earthworks:** | 98 meters (320 feet) |
| **Diameter of stone circle:** | 33 meters (108 feet) |
| **Constructed:** | c. 3000–2000 BCE |
| **Date of Inscription as a UNESCO World Heritage Site:** | 1986 |
| **UNESCO Criteria:** | (i) (ii) (iii) |

# HADRIAN'S WALL
## UNITED KINGDOM

*Widely regarded as one of Rome's wiser emperors, Hadrian (76–138 CE) rose to power following the death of Trajan in 117 CE. With his rule challenged by various rebellions across the empire, he opted—unusually for a Roman leader—not for further expansion, but for consolidation of the empire.*

ON HADRIAN'S DIRECT ORDERS, NEW FORTIFICATIONS WERE ERECTED AT THE LIMITS OF ROMAN TERRITORY—fortifications that the emperor inspected personally, often ignoring pomp and ceremony and eating and sleeping with the common soldiers. The most famous of these is a wall built across the width of Britain, separating Roman territory from the unconquered peoples of the north.

Commonly believed to mark the border of Scotland and England, Hadrian's Wall actually lies completely within England. Counting from its western extreme at Bowness-on-Solway, to its eastern end (the wall begins at Wallsend on the River Tyne), it is up to 110 kilometers (68 miles) from Scotland. Stretching almost from coast to coast—and originally built of turf in places—it runs 117.5 kilometers (73 miles) across the country, its length studded with the ruins of watchtowers, gates, and larger fortresses. Completed around 128 CE, the wall once measured 6 meters (20 feet) high at its highest points and ranged from 3.5 meters (9.8 feet) to 6 meters (20 feet) thick. Earthworks along its length provided further defense while it is thought that at one time the wall itself was plastered and whitewashed, making it a highly visible and massive physical declaration of Roman power. In fact, modern historians believe that the primary purpose of Hadrian's Wall was to psychologically subdue the rebellious local population rather than protect Roman territory from northern marauders. Certainly, it would have been far more expensive to build and garrison than would have been justified by the threat of occasional raids.

*Left:* The remains of the hypocaust (underfloor heating) system at Housesteads (*Vercovicium*) Fort.

*Right:* Fortified milecastles (such as Milecastle 39 seen here), would have been garrisoned year-round and were built every Roman mile along the length of Hadrian's Wall.

The largest—if not the most beautiful—construction ever undertaken by the Roman Empire, the wall has been plundered for its stone over the centuries, considerably diminishing its size. While it was briefly abandoned around 138 CE under Hadrian's successor, Antonius Pius (86–161 CE)—who ordered the building of the Antonine Wall further to the north—Hadrian's famous wall was reoccupied some twenty years later and remained in service for another three centuries. Today it is a cherished part of the British landscape and stands as a potent northern marker of the limits of Ancient Rome.

*Right:* The remains of the Temple of Mithras, near Carrawburgh Roman Fort. Mithras was a Persian deity who was popular with the Roman army from about the first to the fourth century CE.

*Below:* Although the passage of time has reduced the size of the wall, it has become an integral part of the English landscape, running across some of the most beautiful scenery in the British Isles.

### Site information:

| | |
|---|---|
| **Location:** | Northern England, United Kingdom |
| **Type of structure:** | Roman defensive wall |
| **Length:** | 117.5 kilometers (73 miles) |
| **Height:** | Originally between 3.5 meters (11 feet) and 6 meters (20 feet) |
| **Width:** | Originally between 3 meters (9 feet) and 6 meters (20 feet) |
| **Constructed:** | c.122–128 CE |

**Date of Inscription as a UNESCO World Heritage Site:** 1987

**UNESCO Criteria:** (ii) (iii) (iv)

# AFRICA

# LUXOR TEMPLE
## EGYPT

*While it may not have been as large as the sacred site of Thebes, the complex now known as the Temple of Luxor occupies a unique place in Ancient Egyptian history.*

ALIGNED WITH, AND CONNECTED TO, THE LARGER KARNAK TEMPLE COMPLEX BY A 3-KILOMETER (1.8-MILE) AVENUE LINED WITH SPHINXES, it was known to its builders as ipet resyt—the southern sanctuary—and was intimately connected to the divine aspects of kingship for over a millennium. An indication of its importance can be found in Alexander the Great's (356–323 BCE) insistence that he was crowned here when he became pharaoh in 332 BCE after invading the country. Although his actual coronation is thought to have taken place at Memphis, far to the north, a symbolic ritual at the Temple of Luxor would have stamped legitimacy on his reign and been considered the more important of the two rites.

Although the older shrine of Thutmose III and Hatshepsut still found within the temple's precincts predates it, the first stage of the temple's construction took place during the reign of Amenhotep III,

*Below*: Viewed from the Avenue of Sphinxes and lit up at night, the entrance of the Temple of Luxor is flanked by two statues of Ramesses II (there were once six). The twin of the single obelisk that remains in situ can now be found in the Place de la Concorde in Paris.

who ruled from 1386 to about 1351 BCE. Also known as Amenhotep the Magnificent, his long reign was marked by peace, prosperity, and a flowering of art and architecture that is apparent in the superb design and fabulous carved reliefs at Luxor. Later, Ramesses II (ruled 1279–1213 BCE) enlarged the complex and it was later further remodeled (though not extensively), before becoming a shrine to the emperor under Roman rule. Over the years the temple has been robbed of some of its grandeur; for example, only one of the great 25 meter (82 foot) pink granite obelisks remains standing at the temple entrance—its twin stands at the center of the Place de la Concorde in Paris. Even so, what remains of the Temple of Luxor is in excellent condition considering its vast age.

*Opposite page:* Hieroglyph-covered columns in the temple's Hypostyle Hall record the martial victories of Seti I and Ramesses II.

*Below:* Colossal statues of the pharaoh in the Great Court of Ramesses II mark the entrance to the colonnade that joins the court to the Court of Amenhotep III.

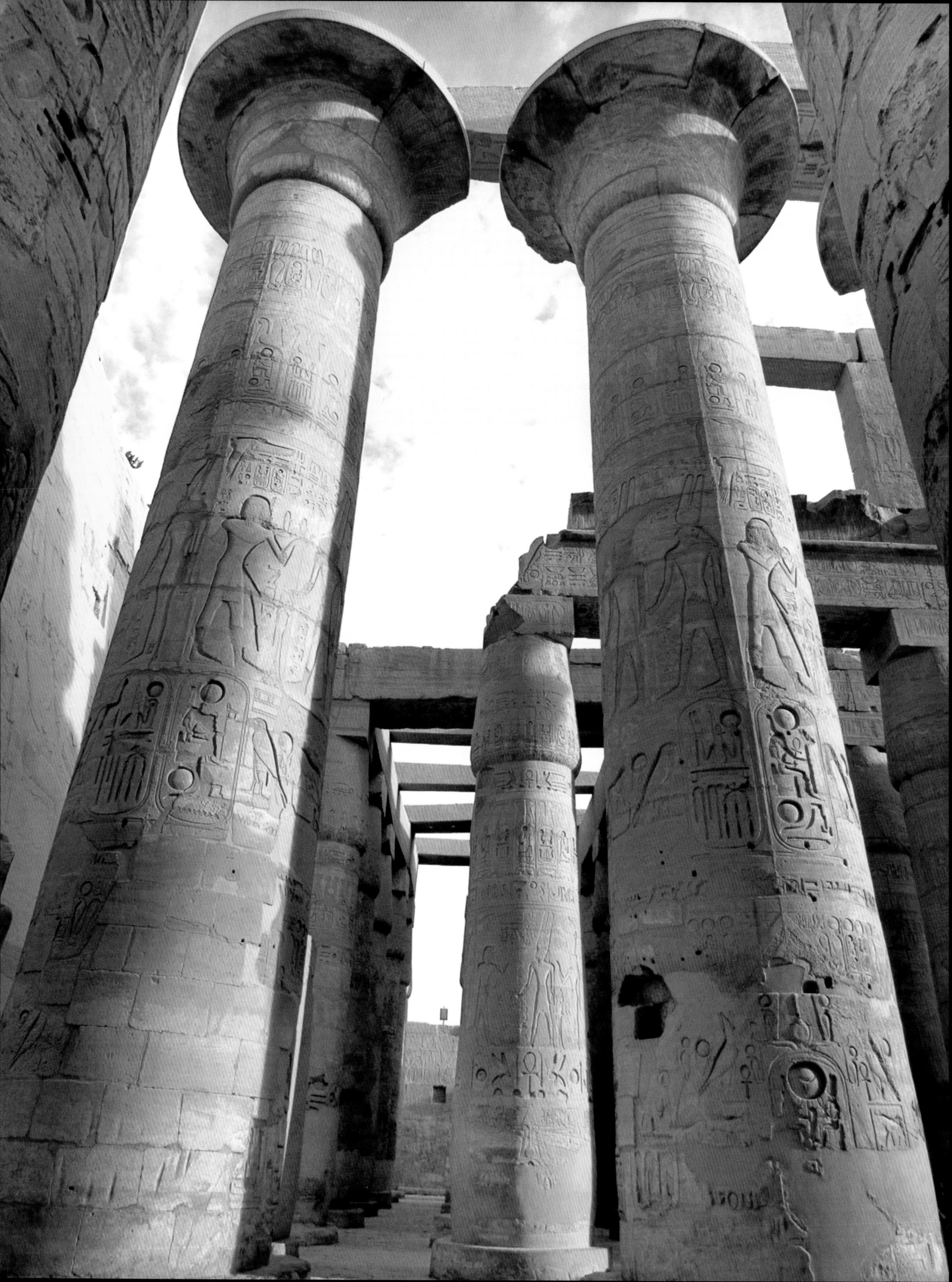

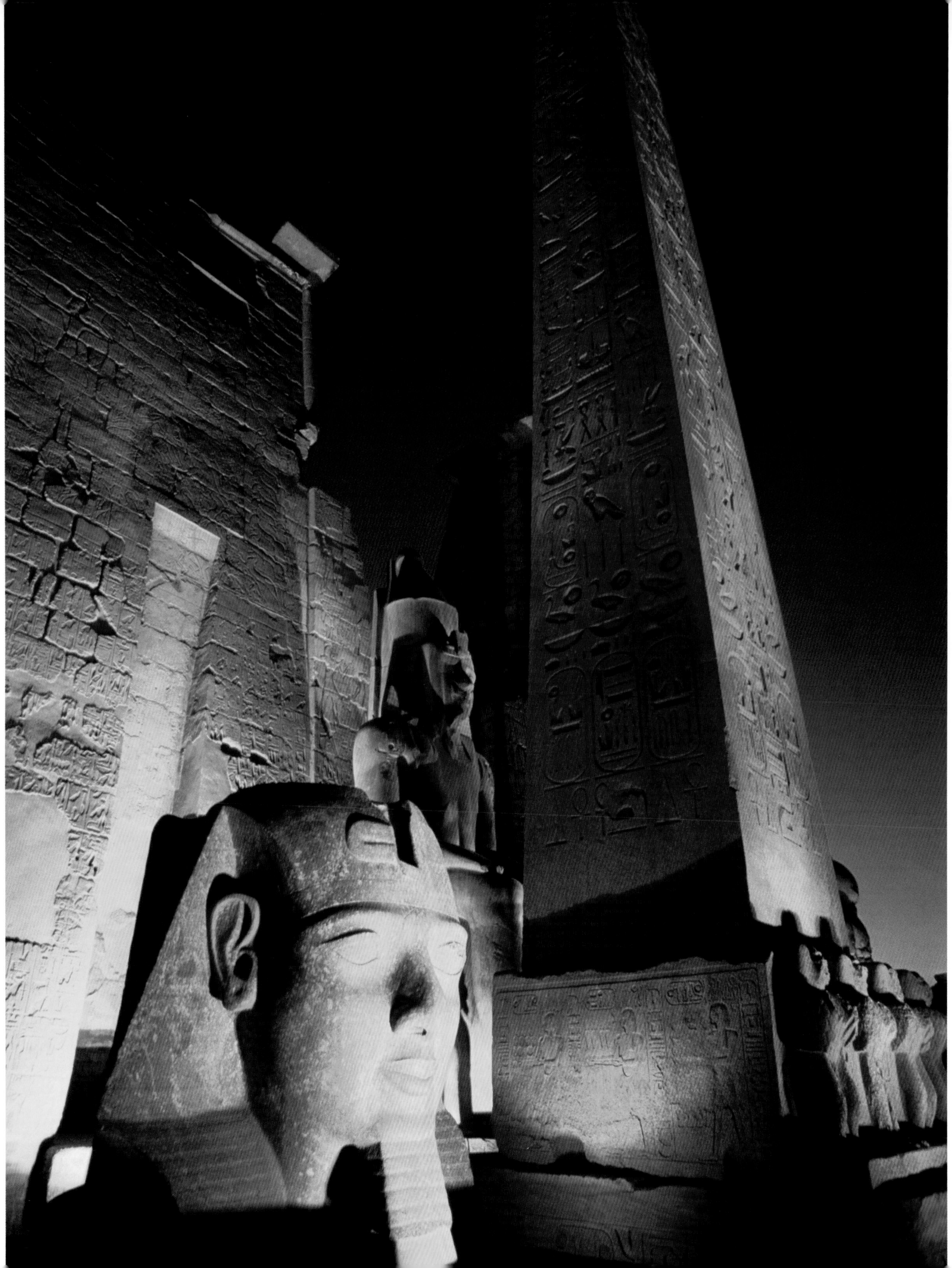

Today's visitors enter from the sphinx-lined avenue through a gate between two monumental towers known as the First Pylon, which record the military victories of Ramesses II (now badly eroded). Outside the gate stands the remaining obelisk, as well as two colossal statues of a seated Ramesses (there were originally six with the four others depicting the pharaoh standing). Within is the peristyle Courtyard of Ramesses II —a courtyard with a surrounding gallery supported by a double row of columns—which contains the shrine of Thutmose III (c. 1481–1425 BCE) and his stepmother, aunt, and co-ruler Hatshepsut (c. 1478–1458 BCE) as well as the remains of an early Christian church that was later converted into a mosque.

From the southern end of the courtyard runs a 100 meter (330 foot) colonnade of massive columns, seven per side, each measuring 19 meters (62 feet) high. Once enclosed and roofed, carved reliefs here celebrate the Festival of Opet (during which statues of Amun, Mut, and Khonsu were paraded here from the Karnak temple) and bear the names of pharaohs including Amenhotep III, Ramesses II, Horemheb, Seti II, and Tutankhamun. This leads into the Court of Amenhotep III, the original entrance to the temple before it was enlarged. Similarly to Ramesses' courtyard, Amenhotep's features a double row of columns around three sides with the Hypostyle Hall—featuring four rows of eight columns—at the southern end.

Beyond the Hypostyle Hall is a complex of chambers leading from the First Antechamber, or the Chamber of the Divine King, where scenes depicting Amenhotep III paying tribute to Amun were plastered over by the Romans and painted with images of the emperor. Early Christians would have been brought here and forced to capitulate to the Roman god-emperor on pain of torture or death. Other rooms include chapels dedicated to Mut (the mother goddess) and Khunsu (god of time) as well as an Offerings Vestibule where the painted reliefs show Amenhotep making ritual offerings—of cattle as well as incense and flowers—to Amun. Behind this is a shrine originally dedicated to Amun, but which was later rededicated to Alexander the Great. During his campaigns of conquest, Alexander often incorporated foreign deities into his own, Hellenistic, belief system, and the reliefs here show him making offerings to the god, whom he would have identified as a representation of Zeus. In a chamber known as the Birth Room are reliefs that encapsulate the temple's purpose. Here, Amenhotep's divine right to rule is asserted, underscored by reliefs showing his mother, Mutemuya, being impregnated by touching fingertips with Amun.

More recently in history, the temple has hosted a church, which later became a mosque. Like so many other ancient sites it has suffered from neglect, vandalism, and robbery as well as the simple passage of time. Even 3,500 years have not managed to eradicate the temple's glory, however. To walk between the monumental towers of the First Pylon is to walk back into Ancient Egyptian history where kings were literally gods on Earth.

*Left*: Hatshepsut's Obelisk in the Temple of Karnak.

*Above*: Close-up of carvings on a wall. The reliefs showing offerings being made to the gods.

| Site information: | |
|---|---|
| **Location:** | Governorate of Qina, Egypt |
| **Type of structure:** | Ancient Egyptian temple complex |
| **Length:** | 190 meters (625 feet) from First Pylon to rear wall |
| **Width:** | 55 meters (180 feet) |
| **Completed:** | c. 2500 BCE (contested) |
| **Date of Inscription as a UNESCO World Heritage Site:** 1979 | |
| **UNESCO Criteria:** | (i) (iii) (vi) |

# PYRAMIDS OF GIZA
## EGYPT

*Igniting the imaginations of millions over the centuries, the construction of the enigmatic Giza pyramids at such an early point in the history of civilization has caused bafflement and wonder for millennia.*

RISING DRAMATICALLY FROM THE SANDS OUTSIDE CAIRO, these breathtaking structures are on a scale that seems beyond the realm of human industry, especially a human industry that was equipped with simple tools of stone and copper. Some people have speculated that encoded into their dimensions are messages from the ancient past written in the universal languages of mathematics and astronomy. Others say that the pyramids are "spiritual batteries" or even alien space ships. The wilder theories can easily be debunked by careful research, but, even so, there are mysteries about the Giza Pyramids that provoke fierce argument to this day.

Surrounded by smaller satellite pyramids and temples, and with the Sphinx just a short distance away, the three main pyramids are widely accepted as the tombs of three pharaohs. The Great Pyramid—the only Wonder of the Ancient World still extant—is said to have

been the resting place of Khufu (also known by the Greek form of his name, Cheops). Directly diagonal to it is the very slightly less imposing pyramid of his son Khafre (Chephren to the Greeks), while offset from the diagonal—in a manner that mirrors Orion's Belt in the Orion constellation—is the smaller pyramid of Khafre's son, Menkaure (Menkaura). The pyramids' construction is dated to an intense building period of about eighty years, between c. 2560 and 2480 BCE.

Interestingly, if the pyramids were used as tombs, they are tombs unlike those of any other king or queen of Egypt. Although artifacts related to the three pharaohs have been found among the surrounding pyramids and temples, the walls of the main pyramids' internal chambers were not carved or painted with ornate hieroglyphs and tributes to the dead pharaoh as found in other tombs. For example, the only reference to Khufu in the Great Pyramid can be found in some

"building site graffiti" in an obscure upper chamber. Why a great king would build such a vast and expensive monument to himself and then neglect to have even his name carved into it remains unexplained.

All three pyramids contain or contained sarcophagi (the Pyramid of Menkaure once held a highly ornamented sarcophagus but this was lost during a shipwreck while being transported to London), but none were ever found to contain the mummified remains of the pharaohs. Indeed, when Caliph Abdullah Al Ma'mun tunneled into the Great Pyramid in 820 CE he found it completely empty. While it was believed that the pyramid had already been looted at an earlier period, it seems strange that there was not so much as a broken pottery shard to suggest that the pyramid had ever contained the rich funerary objects associated with a royal tomb.

Adding to the mystery, the Great Pyramid in particular was clearly planned along sophisticated astronomical and mathematical principles. In fact, it has been described as a mathematical symphony in stone, with various researchers pointing out that its dimensions incorporate both pi and phi (the golden ratio number beloved by architects and artists), both of which are usually agreed to have been "discovered" by Greek mathematicians about 2,000 years later. When Sir Isaac Newton needed to calculate the circumference of the Earth, he sent a man to measure the Great Pyramid. The calculations Newton made using those numbers only proved to be wrong because his assistant had failed to take into

account debris at the base. Other mathematicians say they have used the dimensions encoded in the Great Pyramid to calculate other important numbers, up to and including the speed of light although this is—obviously—highly contested.

Astronomically, too, the Great Pyramid presents us with enigmas. It is aligned almost perfectly to North, South, East, and West, while shafts running through the structure would have aligned to stars in the Orion and Sirius constellations at the time of its building. Again, the reason for incorporating such features into a tomb is unclear, though the Ancient Egyptians had a complex religious system in which both these constellations were important. It may be that such a shaft was intended to guide the pharaoh's soul towards the stars.

Questions regarding why the Giza pyramids were built to such exact specifications go on and on (there are numerous books on the subject) but these are not the only questions to cause disagreement among Egyptologists. The question of how they were built has been equally controversial. During construction granite stones—some weighing eighty tonnes—had to be transported from Aswan, 800 km (500 miles) away, then perfectly shaped, lifted, and positioned with millimeter accuracy. After the initial construction had finished, the pyramids were then fitted with polished white limestone facing blocks (few of which survive today) giving them a sleek, highly reflective appearance. The Great Pyramid alone used 2.3 million blocks in its

construction. Assuming the twenty-year construction time is correct and that work continued twenty-four hours a day, 365 days of the year, this means blocks were placed and checked at an average rate of one every three or four minutes. How this was done is a problem that has baffled visitors since ancient times. In the fifth century BCE, the Greek historian Herodotus, who visited the site, wrote of a complicated system of specially constructed barges and causeways that took years to build. The workforce was "enslaved" from the local population with 100,000 people working a three-month shift before being replaced by another 100,000, and so on. This suggests that work was on some sort of taxation system. More recently, archaeologists have suggested that the project might have involved even larger numbers of the population during gaps in the agricultural cycle, and that workers were fed, clothed, and cared for by the pharaoh during these times. If true, the idea of such a staggering effort leads us back to why. Why go to such incredible lengths and then fail to mark his own name somewhere inside the tomb?

Perhaps future archaeologists will help unlock the secrets of the pyramids, but however they were built, and for what reason, the Pyramids of Giza certainly represent the phenomenal effort of a sophisticated culture that was skilled in mathematics, astronomy, architecture, stone working, and construction, to a degree that seems almost beyond possibility. Whatever else they might tell us, the continued existence of these puzzling monuments after 4,500 years of robbery, earthquakes, and human conflict reminds us how much knowledge of the past has been lost to us.

*Previous pages:* A panorama of the Giza pyramids taken from the south. In the foreground to the left are the pyramids of queens. Behind them, from left to right, are those of Menkaure, Khafre, and Khufu (the Great Pyramid).

*Above:* The Great Pyramid from above. When first built, the structure would have been encased in polished white stone and probably capped with semiprecious stone or even gold. Accounts report that the Great Pyramid's cap was already missing by around the time of Christ. As it is highly unlikely that the pyramid remained unfinished, it seems that it was stolen in the distant past.

## Site information:

**Location:** Governorate of Giza, Egypt

**Type of structure:** Funerary monuments. The Great Pyramid is a Wonder of the Ancient World

**Completed:** c. 2500 BCE (contested)

**Date of Inscription as a UNESCO World Heritage Site:** 1979

**UNESCO Criteria:** (i) (iii) (vi)

### Khufu's Pyramid (Great Pyramid)

**Completed:** c. 2560 BCE

**Height (ancient):** 146.5 meters (481 feet)

**Height (contemporary):** 138.8 meters (455 feet)

**Base:** 230.4 meters (756 feet)

### Khafre's Pyramid

**Completed:** c. 2530 BCE

**Height (ancient):** 143.5 meters (471 feet)

**Height (contemporary):** 136.4 meters (448 feet)

**Base:** 215.3 meters (706 feet)

### Menkaure's Pyramid

**Completed:** c. 2490 BCE

**Height:** 65 meters (213 feet)

**Base:** 102.2 x 104.6 meters (335 x 343 feet)

# THE SPHINX
## EGYPT

*Popularly associated with riddles, the Great Sphinx of Giza does indeed represent unsolvable enigmas:
who built it, when, and why?*

NO ONE EVEN KNOWS WHAT ITS BUILDERS CALLED IT—THE NAME SPHINX DERIVES FROM A HUMAN-HEADED, winged lion from Greek mythology and wasn't used to describe the statue until thousands of years after it had been carved. None of the hieroglyphs in the surrounding tombs mention it, and the few ancient stelae that do mark its existence are either incomplete or contradictory. Today, most Egyptologists agree that it dates to the reign of Khafre (c. 2570 BCE) but the Sphinx's human face does not match other representations of the pharaoh. Neither does it match the rest of the statue in its proportions, leading some to wonder whether the Sphinx originally had a lion's or jackal's head that was re-carved at a later date.

One of the world's largest statues, the Sphinx was carved from the limestone bedrock. Measuring 73 meters (238 feet) long from paw to tail, 19 meters (63 feet) wide at the rear haunches, and over 20 meters (66 feet) high to the top of its head, it's a short walk from the pyramids, directly facing the rising sun during the March and September equinoxes every year.

Weathered by the passing of millennia and deprived of its nose by unknown vandals (various tales blame an overzealous Muslim leader, Napoleonic, or British troops), the Sphinx was buried beneath the desert sands for many centuries until it was dug out between 1925 and 1936.

Traces of paint still clinging to parts of the statue suggest that at one time it was brightly painted.

Today, the Sphinx provokes fierce argument among academics and fringe theorists. The geologist Robert M. Soloch believes that water erosion patterns on the statue prove the Sphinx existed at a time when the area experienced heavy rainfall and, therefore, means that it must have been carved at least 3,000 years before Khafre constructed his pyramid close by. Others, such as Graham Hancock, have suggested that, together with the pyramids, the Sphinx is part of a complex that marks the heavens as they appeared in 10,500 BCE, the end of the last Ice Age and a time of deluge and cataclysm. For Hancock, the Sphinx's existence—and that of many other ancient monuments—points to the involvement of a high civilization (mysteriously almost completely destroyed) that was attempting to pass on its knowledge.

Most historians agree, however, that the Sphinx was carved around the same time as the pyramids were erected. The respected American archaeologist, Mark Lehrer, who has spent decades at the location, believes that the whole site with its temples and pyramids was connected to the sun god Ra, and may have been built in an effort to harness the god's regenerative powers, powering the dead pharaoh's soul back to eternal life in the heavens.

*Above:* Now without its face and beard, and unpainted, the face of the Sphinx represents a mystery. Most Egyptologists agree that it is the face of Khafre, but experts argue it does not resemble other depictions of the pharaoh. Adding to the mystery, others have suggested that the head is too small for the Sphinx's body and the gigantic sculpture might once have had a lion's head.

*Right:* An aerial view of the Sphinx. At the tips of its front paws is the Sphinx Temple, which is thought to have been built using blocks quarried during construction work on the Sphinx.

*Below left:* The Sphinx measures 73 metres (238 feet) from paws to tail, making it the largest monumental sculpture of Ancient Egypt, as well as one of the oldest.

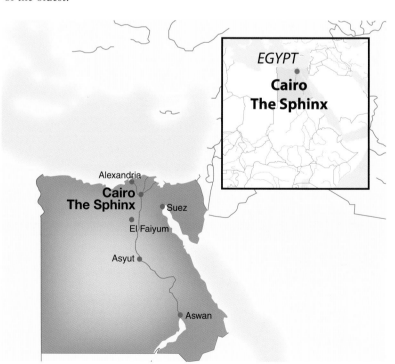

### Site information:

| | |
|---|---|
| Location: | Governorate of Giza, Egypt |
| Type of structure: | Funeray monument |
| Length: | 73 meters (238 feet) |
| Width: | 19 meters (62.6 feet) |
| Height: | 20.21 meters (66.3 feet) |
| Completed: | c. 2500 BCE (contested) |

**Date of Inscription as a UNESCO World Heritage Site:** 1979

**UNESCO Criteria:** (i) (iii) (vi)

# ANCIENT THEBES
## EGYPT

*Once the largest city on Earth with a population of about 80,000, ancient Thebes was the seat of pharaohs and high priests—the hub of Ancient Egypt during the New Kingdom period which lasted five centuries, between 1570 and 1069 BCE, and a religious center for centuries after that.*

*Below:* The Mortuary Temple of Hatshepsut, a female pharaoh who reigned between c. 1478 and 1458 BCE. Architecturally distinguished by its three colonnaded terraces, the temple is considered one of the finest of Ancient Egypt's monuments.

A DAZZLING CITY OF WEALTH AND ARCHITECTURAL WONDERS, THEBES WAS REFERRED TO SEVERAL TIMES IN THE BIBLE AS NO-AMON (or, simply, No), and by Homer as Thebai in his epic, *The Iliad*. The Greeks also coined another name for it: Diospolis Magna, "the great city of the gods."

Thebes' own citizens knew the city as Wase or Wo'se. To them it was sacred to Amun, the king of the gods. Accordingly, they lavished temples and monuments on the city. Within its ancient 93 square kilometer (36 square mile) boundary, or nearby, stand some of the most impressive remains of Ancient Egyptian culture: a great avenue of sphinxes, palaces, colossal temples, and tombs including the Valley of Kings and the Valley of Queens.

Although we shall look at the Temple of Luxor in more detail over the following pages, many of Thebes' ancient sites could easily have replaced it in this book. Among the most important is the Temple Complex of Amun at nearby Karnak. Covering an area of 1,500 meters by 800 meters (5,000 feet by 2,600 feet), it is the largest religious edifice ever built and remains breathtaking. Mirroring the ancient city's rise to prominence, it is thought that the complex was added to and enlarged over at least 2,000 years.

Close to the Valley of Kings rise the colonnaded terraces of the Mortuary Temple of Pharaoh Hatshepsut—mother of Thutmose II, who ruled Egypt for some twenty-two years. Described as one of the "incomparable monuments of Ancient Egypt," its simple, severe lines still strike today's visitors as distinctly modern. Famously, the valleys containing the richly ornamented tombs of kings, queens, and nobles have provided a wealth of information about Ancient Egyptian religious belief and funeral rites.

During the reign of Ramesses II (1279–1213 BCE) Egypt's capital moved to Per-Ramesses. Thebes, however, remained an important religious site—and base of the formidable priesthood—throughout Ancient Egypt's history. Sacked by the Assyrians in 666 BCE, and devastated by Roman forces in the first century CE, its inhabitants abandoned the ruined city, leaving it to become an early tourist site and for future archaeologists to unravel its glorious history.

*Above:* This sculptural detail from Hatshepsut's temple depicts the goddess Hathor, who was said to have suckled the infant Hatshepsut.

*Left:* Detail from the red granite sarcophagus of Ramesses III, which was found in his tomb in the Valley of the Kings. It shows the goddess Nephthys protecting the pharaoh and the passage of the Underworld.

*Opposite page, above:* Also found in the Valley of the Kings are the two statues known as the Colossi of Memnon. Standing 18 metres (60 feet) high, the colossi depict the pharaoh Amenhotep III (ruled c. 1391–53 BCE).

*Opposite page, below:* Ruins at the Temple of Karnak. The complex includes numerous temples, chapels, and other monuments and remains the second largest religious site ever built (after Angkor Wat).

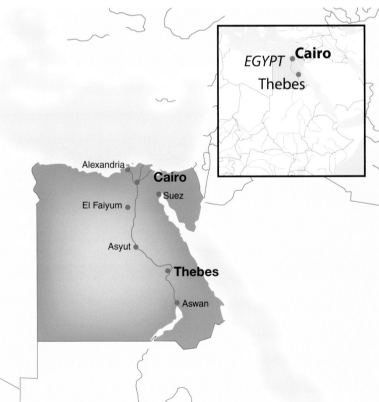

| Site information: | |
| --- | --- |
| **Location:** | Governorate of Qina, Egypt |
| **Type of structure:** | Ancient Egyptian city and religious hub |
| **Area:** | 93 square kilometers (36 square miles) |
| **Completed:** | c. 2000-667 BCE |
| **Date of Inscription as a UNESCO World Heritage Site:** | 1979 |
| **UNESCO Criteria:** | (i) (iii) (vi) |

# ABU SIMBEL
## EGYPT

*An iconic symbol of Ancient Egypt, the two temples of Abu Simbel stand on the River Nile, close to the border with Sudan.*

THE TEMPLES CELEBRATE RAMESSES II'S VICTORY OVER THE HITTITES AT THE BATTLE OF KADESH, as well as his own divinity and the pharaoh's love of his favorite wife, Nefertari. The temples would also have served to impress the pharaoh's power upon Egypt's southern neighbors. Carved into the hillside between 1264 BCE and 1244 BCE, they had already been long abandoned and forgotten by the time of Christ and lay almost completely buried beneath the sand for many centuries. Rediscovered by the Swiss explorer Johann Ludwig Burckhardt (1784–1817) in 1813, legend says the site was subsequently named after the local boy who guided him to their location.

Four monumental statues of Ramesses II guard the entrance to the Great Temple. Each of these vast statues measures 20 meters (65 feet) tall, although one has been damaged by an earthquake (its head and upper body now lie at the pharaoh's feet). They show Ramesses in a serene, seated position, wearing the Double Crown of Upper and Lower Egypt. The faces show the skill of Egyptian craftsmen who incorporated perfect symmetry into their work using the most basic of tools. At the pharaoh's knees are smaller statues of the royal family, above the doorway to the temple is a carving of Ramesses honoring the falcon-headed Re-Horakhty, while beneath his feet are reliefs depicting Ramesses victories.

*Above:* Sunrise at Abu Simbel. To the left is the Temple of Ramesses II. The smaller statues on the right mark the entrance to the Small Temple of Nefertari, the pharaoh's favorite wife.

*Opposite page:* The statues outside Nefertari's temple were unique among Ancient Egyptian monuments at the time they were built. It is thought that this was the first time that a pharaoh's wife was depicted the same size as the king himself. Normally, she would have been shown at around knee height, as can be seen at the neighboring temple.

### Site information:

| | |
|---|---|
| **Location:** | Governorate of Aswan, Egypt |
| **Type of structure:** | Ancient Egyptian temple complex |
| **Area:** | 3.75 square kilometers (1.45 square miles) |
| **Completed:** | 1264-1244 BCE |
| **Date of Inscription as a UNESCO World Heritage Site:** | 1979 |
| **UNESCO Criteria:** | (i) (ii) (vi) |

Within the temple lies a grand hall, which features eight massive pillars, again carved to depict Ramesses, as well as a wealth of carved reliefs that boast of his victories. From here passages lead away to smaller rooms showing the pharaoh making offerings to the gods, and to a second hall, with four pillars and reliefs emphasizing the mutual affection between Ramesses and the gods. Beyond is an inner sanctuary, perfectly aligned so that at sunrise on February 22 and October 22 each year light pierces the entire length of the temple—55 meters (180 feet)—to illuminate statues of the gods Ra, Amun, and Ramesses himself. A fourth statue—Ptah, god of the Underworld—lies forever in darkness.

The second temple is smaller—only 28 meters (92 feet) in length—and dedicated to Nefertari, its entrance flanked by six 10 meter (33 foot) standing figures—four of Ramesses, two of his wife with royal children standing beside them. Most unusually, Nefertari is depicted as the same size as her husband, rather than as the usual knee-high figure dictated by Ancient Egyptian convention. Inside, the temple is decorated with scenes of Ramesses and Nefertari making offerings to the gods.

Between 1964 and 1968, the entire temple complex was cut into huge blocks and moved 200 meters (660 feet) back from the water's edge to rescue it from rising waters created by the Aswan High Dam—an unrivaled feat of archaeology and engineering that rescued Ramesses' monumental tribute to his own glory and to his love for Nefertari for future generations.

*Opposite page, above:* Twice a year (on dates that are believed to mark the pharaoh's birthday and coronation day) morning light pierces the depths of the Temple of Ramesses II to illuminate three statues. The fourth statue—that of Ptah, god of the Underworld—remains in the dark.

*Opposite page, below left:* Within the pharaoh's temple, great statues in the Hypostyle Hall depict Ramesses II, while wall paintings celebrate his victories.

*Opposite page, below right:* One of the most famous sights of Ancient Egypt, the four colossal statues of Ramesses II that stand guard outside the entrance to the pharaoh's temple.

*Below:* This photograph of the Hypostyle Hall gives some idea of the temple's awe-inspiring architecture. The statues of Ramesses on the left wear the White Crown of Upper Egypt. Those on the right wear the Double Crown of Upper and Lower Egypt.

# MEROË PYRAMIDS
## SUDAN

*Spread across the ancient Kingdom of Kush at the sites of Meroë, el-Kurru, and Nuri are more than 250 pyramids.*

RELATIVELY UNKNOWN AND OFTEN CALLED THE FORGOTTEN PYRAMIDS, the distinctive Meroë pyramids are steeply angled with relatively small bases and often accompanied by adjoining H-shaped temples for offerings. They are smaller than their Egyptian counterparts—ranging from 6 meters (20 feet) to 30 meters (98 feet) in height—but served a similar purpose as royal tombs. Clearly influenced by the culture of Egypt, (although in comparison, there are 120

pyramids throughout Egypt), which Kush conquered between 712–657 BCE, these structures speak of a people who may have assimilated ideas from elsewhere but whose own culture diverged from that of Egypt in many important ways. For instance, many of the tombs appear to have once contained warrior queens as well as kings.

The largest collection of pyramids is found at the old Kushite capital of Meroë, once a crossroads of ancient trade routes and

*Right:* Today, the pyramids of Meroë are in various states of repair. In the 19th century the explorer Guiseppe Ferlini blew the tops off at least forty while searching for hidden gold.

*Below:* A stunning panorama across the Sahara Desert. The distinctively steep-sided Meroë pyramids were often built with a small H-shaped shrine where offerings could be left.

now about 100 kilometers (62 miles) north of modern Khartoum. Within a short distance of the River Nile stand around 200 tombs, of which fifty were royal pyramids. Cremated or mummified, the rulers of Kush were interred in sarcophagi along with their valuables (and sometimes servants and animals) like their earlier Egyptian counterparts. With interiors decorated with hieroglyphs and reliefs, the tombs demonstrate the early strength of Egyptian ideas

that were eventually melded into and then eclipsed by indigenous culture. Hieroglyphs, for instance, were eventually replaced by an entirely new writing system known as Meroitic, which has yet to be completely translated.

All of the pyramids were, sadly, plundered at some point in antiquity but archaeologists have unearthed broken weapons and pieces of furniture, as well as pottery fragments and bronze and silver vessels that

*Above:* Although the people of Kush built smaller pyramids than their northern neighbors, the Egyptian influence is obvious both in their design and in the carved reliefs that adorn the interiors.

*Left:* The pyramids of Meroë include many that contained kings and—notably—queens. This example is in a remarkably good state of repair.

speak of a people who were well connected by trade to Greece and forty while searching for the golden treasure mentioned in local folklore.

Around 330 CE, this once rich and powerful kingdom that traded war elephants to its neighbors suffered a steep decline after being conquered by the Aksumites. The use of Meroitic ceased and desertification of the landscape contributed to the collapse of ancient Kush. Its elegant pyramids, which look so strange to eyes more used to the squatter structures of the Egyptians, remind us how much remains to be discovered about a civilization that assimilated the ideas of others and worked them into a culture that was clearly unique.

Meroë Pyramids
**Khartoum** •
*SUDAN*

Ad Damir

**Meroë Pyramids** •

• **Khartoum**

Kusti •

### Site information:

| | |
|---|---|
| **Location:** | Sudan |
| **Type of structure:** | Ancient Kushite pyramid tombs |
| **Height:** | Up to 30 meters (98 feet) |
| **Base:** | Up to 8 meters (26 feet) square |
| **Completed:** | c. 720 BCE–c. 300 CE |
| **Date of Inscription as a UNESCO World Heritage Site:** | 2011 |
| **UNESCO Criteria:** | (ii) (iii) (iv) (v) |

# CARTHAGE
## TUNISIA

*In his epic poem* Aeneid, *the Roman poet Virgil tells how the city of Carthage was founded by the legendary queen Dido (also known as Elissa), daughter of the King of Tyre.*

FLEEING HER FATHER'S CITY AFTER A DISPUTE OVER SUCCESSION, DIDO ARRIVED AT THE HILL KNOWN AS BYRSA and offered to buy from the local chieftan as much land as could be covered by an oxhide. Cutting the hide into thin strips she used them to encircle the summit and claimed it as her own. In truth, the city is thought to have been founded by Phoenician settlers sometime in the ninth century BCE, but the fact that it had—by Roman times—a well-established mythology of its own, gives some indication of the city's importance in the ancient European world

Once the heart of a wealthy and powerful trading empire that dominated the Mediterranean, Carthage is probably most famous for the three Punic wars (*Punicus* meaning Carthaginian in Latin) it fought with upstart Rome between 264 and 146 BCE, during which time Hannibal made his epic journey across the Alps. Finally defeated, the city was razed to the ground by the Romans as punishment. Although there is no evidence to support the story, it was said that even its earth was salted so nothing would grow there again.

In fact, the Romans swiftly rebuilt Carthage and by the first century CE it was again a powerful city—the hub of Rome's African territories, a major trading port, and the third largest city in the empire after Rome and Alexandria.

Today, Carthage is a city of layers. Over its ancient heritage lie Roman remains; later, the city became an important Christian center and a Byzantine outpost. Now, it is a beautiful suburb of Tunis with a craggy landscape, a view over the Mediterranean, and—more importantly—a major archaeological site that provides a window into the distant past. First surveyed in the early nineteenth century, subsequent finds here have uncovered many surprises, including a cooling system for horses and charioteers at the city's impressive circus, as well as caches of mixed infant and animal bones that suggest child sacrifice was practiced in ancient Carthage.

Once protected by a 40 kilometer (25 mile) long, 13 meter (43 foot) high wall studded with defensive towers, the city was an ancient marvel and a powerhouse of culture. Evidence of Carthage's former importance are scattered around the modern streets, but the most important archaeological site is undoubtedly the ancient acropolis of Byrsa, where Dido is said to have laid her oxhide strips. Destroyed and rebuilt by the Romans, this was once the administrative heart of the city, and still boasts the remains of temples, a library, and a forum dating to Roman times as well as the ruins of an earlier residential neighborhood—the Punic Quarter—that dates to around 300 BCE. Buried by the invaders,

*Above:* This Carthaginian mosaic dates from the city's period of Roman rule and depicts a Vestal Virgin.

*Right:* The ruins at the Punic Quarter on Byrsa were lucky to escape the widespread destruction visited on the city at the end of the Punic Wars. Among the most archaeologically important of Carthage's treasures, they offer a rare glimpse of the ancient, pre-Roman city.

the pre-Roman streets speak of an orderly people who built multi-story homes with ground-floor shops to a strict grid plan.

Below the old citadel, on the coast, a number of ruins and a small museum mark the site of the Punic Ports, the base of the great warships that ensured Carthage's mastery of the Mediterranean and the source of the city's great wealth. From here, Carthaginian merchants sailed as far south as Nigeria on the western coast of Africa and as far north as Cornwall, England. Said to have been big enough to harbor more than 200 ships, the commercial fleet would have moored in the rectangular port area that lay open to the sea, while the military ships had access to an impressive "secret" circular port that contained shipyards and slipways.

It is thought that the religious culture in Punic Carthage appropriated the traditions of other Mediterranean peoples (notably the Greeks) but pre-eminent among them would have been the gods of the ancient Phoenicians, the city's first colonists. Unearthed in 1921, the Sanctuary of Tophet lay for centuries beneath later Roman structures and presents evidence of a darker side to Carthaginian history. More than 20,000 urns were

*Right:* West of Byrsa Hill is Carthage's Roman amphitheater, which dates to the first century CE.

*Below:* Today, little remains of the Antonine baths, but the spectacular setting hints at the luxury they offered to fortunate citizens.

discovered here containing the bones of very young babies and children who are believed to have been sacrificed to the goddess Tanit and the ram-horned god Baal Hammon. Modern dating techniques indicate that the majority of these deaths took place between the fourth and second centuries BCE—a time of war for the Carthaginians when every effort would have been made to secure divine help.

Elsewhere are remnants dating from the city's period of Roman rule befitting their enormous importance to the empire. These include a large circus for chariot racing, styled after Circus Maximus in Rome and measuring over 470 meters (1,550 feet) with seating for around 45,000 spectators. Carthage also had a Roman theater (still in use) as well as an amphitheater, a sophisticated water system, and the splendid Antonine Baths, built with spectacular sea views during the reign of Emperor Antonius Pius (ruled 138–161 CE).

Roman might, however, could not completely blot out Carthage's more distant history forever, and the fragments that remain paint a fascinating picture of a city that rose to supreme power, fell, and then rose again.

*Above left:* Today, the marks of ancient Roman civilization are far more extensive than those of the pre-Roman Punic Carthaginians. These Latin-inscribed pieces of masonry were once part of a bath complex.

*Below left:* Another villa dating back to Roman times. It is now in a better state of repair, and is known as Des Voilieres.

*Above left:* The ruins of a Roman villa. Like Ephesus to the east, Carthage was an important Mediterranean trading hub and counted many wealthy citizens amongst its population.

*Above:* Eerie monuments at the sanctuary of Tophet, dedicated to the gods Baal Hammon and Tanit. The site contains many infant graves, which has led to speculation that child sacrifice was practiced by the pre-Roman Carthaginians.

| Site information: | |
|---|---|
| **Location:** | District of Tunis, Tunisia |
| **Type of structure:** | Ancient city |
| **Area:** | 6.16 square kilometers (2.38 square miles) |
| **Completed:** | c. 800 BCE |
| **Date of Inscription as a UNESCO World Heritage Site:** | 1979 |
| **UNESCO Criteria:** | (ii) (iii) (vi) |

# MIDDLE EAST
# AND ASIA

# PETRA
## JORDAN

*Approached through a long and dim, deep and narrow gorge called the Siq, the sudden sight of Petra at the end of the passage was undoubtedly one of the most stunning views the ancient world had to offer.*

CHISELED FROM THE REGION'S RUGGED CLIFFS, PETRA REMAINS A SECRET CITY THAT GLOWS SOFTLY PINK IN THE SUNLIGHT, its artfully cut façades a millennia-old testament to the engineering skill and design genius of its builders.

Known to its earliest inhabitants as Raqmu, Petra was established as the capital city of the Nabataean Arabs around 312 BCE, and swiftly developed from a simple stronghold into an important convergence point on trade routes that crossed from east to west and from south Arabia to the north. Out of necessity, the people of this arid part of the world became experts at harvesting water—building dams and reservoirs to create a man-made oasis. Evidence of the Nabataeans' sophisticated water engineering can still be seen throughout Petra. Channels and clay pipe networks ran everywhere in the city from underground cisterns that carefully stored every possible drop of rainwater as well as water from springs. At Petra, passing caravans of merchants could purchase water, food and—just as importantly—safe passage along dangerous roads that carried luxuries from the east to the lucrative markets of Greece, Rome, and Egypt. A city of incense, silks, spices, and perfume, during the first century BCE and the first century CE, Petra became a place where fortunes were made and cultures mingled—a true cultural crossroads.

Petra's citizens spent their newfound wealth on religious offerings (inscriptions detailing generous donations of silver and gold can still be seen), elegant colonnaded streets, and imposing tombs, which were cut into the iron-rich pink sandstone and stood alongside grand homes, banquet halls, and shrines. The city's most famous building is, in fact, a tomb and the first sight to greet visitors as they reach the end of the Siq, it was built as a mausoleum for the Nabataean King Aretas III (ruled 87–62 BCE). The king was a noted enthusiast of Greek art and the design of his resting place reflects his passion. Standing 40 meters (130 feet) high, the façade features two levels of Greek-inspired columns and porticos as well as carved figures of Nabataean and Greek gods. Now known as the Treasury (or *Al-Khazneh* in Arabic), the building derives its name from folktales that tell of bandits hiding their loot in

*Right:* The entrance to Petra is a 1.2-kilometer (0.75-mile) natural gorge known as the Siq—meaning "the shaft."

*Opposite page:* At the end of the Siq, visitors arrive at Petra's most famous sight. Known as the Treasury, the Al-Khazneh is a mausoleum carved directly into the pink cliff face.

the huge urn that stands at the center of the higher level. Although the feature is actually solid sandstone, it is scarred by bullet holes made by Bedouins hoping to shatter it, allowing the fabled riches to pour out.

While the Treasury's position at the entrance to Petra makes it the most visually arresting, the city actually contains over 500 tombs, including a further four royal tombs that stand opposite a Greek-style theater that would have seated 3,000 spectators. Known as the Urn Tomb (the largest of the four), the Corinthian Tomb, the Silk Tomb, and the Palace Tomb, and although none are well-preserved it is still easy to imagine how they would have looked when Petra was a bustling city.

Now heavily weathered, the Silk Tomb is still a particularly fine example. Smaller than the Treasury, its façade was carved into a part of the cliff that features beautiful bands of swirling color, giving it a unique and dramatic appearance. Elsewhere, the Palace Tomb is reported to have been directly inspired by Nero's Golden Palace in Rome. Another famous tomb is hidden away in the rocks above the city: the Al-Dier Monastery, at 50 meters (165 feet) wide and 45 meters (148 feet) tall, this ancient tomb dates to the third century BCE and was similar in design to the Treasury. Crosses carved into the walls here suggest that it may have been used for Christian worship in later times and certainly gave the mausoleum its common name.

*Above:* Slightly to the left of center in this photograph is Petra's largest tomb. Known as the Urn Tomb, it dates to around 70 CE and is thought to have been the mausoleum of King Malchus II.

*Right:* A view of Petra's theater, built in the style of the Ancient Greeks, taken from the mouth of a cave.

Leading away from the Street of Façades a pathway winds upwards to the High Place of Sacrifice where offerings were once made to the Nabataean gods Dushara and al-Uzza. Offering spectacular views of the craggy landscape, this platform in the cliffs stands about 170 meters (560 feet) above ground level and, like the tombs, was carved from the rock face, leaving two 6 meter (20 foot) obelisks in place. Animal (and possibly human) sacrifices would have been made at the altar, the blood draining away in specially cut channels. Another path leads from here to an area known as the Wadi a-Farasa, which boasts more tombs as well as the Garden Temple complex, where the ancient citizens used their irrigation prowess to bring a blaze of color to the desert.

Petra's fortunes declined under Roman rule and the city suffered an earthquake that devastated the water system in 363 CE. By the Middle Ages the city was all but forgotten. However, interest in Petra was revived after it was visited by the explorer Johan Ludwig Burckhardt (who also discovered Abu Simbel) in 1812. Teams of archaeologists began exploring the city during the twentieth century. While much of its history remains to be uncovered, Petra is now recognized as one of the brightest, and most beautiful, jewels of the ancient world. As one of the New Seven Wonders of the World and a UNESCO World Heritage Site it is heavily protected and easily Jordan's biggest tourist attraction.

*Left:* Side by side, the Corinthian Tomb (to the right of the photograph) and the Palace Tomb (left). The Palace Tomb is believed to have been inspired by Emperor Nero's palace in Rome, now the site of the Colosseum.

*Below left:* Dating to around the first century CE, the Al-Dier Monastery is similar in design to the Treasury and was probably originally a temple though it may later have been used as a Christian church or hermitage.

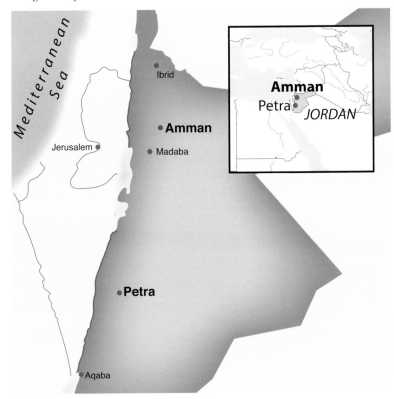

*Above:* No vehicles are allowed within Petra but today's tourists can climb the steps to the High Place of Sacrifice on the back of a donkey.

**Site information:**

| | |
|---|---|
| **Location:** | Ma'an Governorate, Jordan |
| **Type of structure:** | Ancient Nabataean city and trading hub |
| **Area:** | 260 square kilometers (100 square miles) |
| **Completed:** | c. Third century BCE–c. seventh century CE |
| **Date of Inscription as a UNESCO World Heritage Site:** | 1985 |
| **UNESCO Criteria:** | (i) (iii) (iv) |

# PERSEPOLIS
## IRAN

*Originally known as Parsa—meaning, simply, Persia—the ancient fortress citadel of Persepolis was the heart of a mighty empire, a seat of kings, and a palace of mythical riches.*

PARTLY CUT INTO THE MOUNTAIN RUH-E-RAHMET, THE SERIES OF TERRACES, WALLS, AND HIGH RAMPARTS OF PERSEPOLIS were thought to be all but invincible before the city fell to Alexander the Great in 330 BCE. Its conqueror then committed one of history's greatest acts of vandalism by looting the king's palace then torching it. What riches he plundered remain a mystery—though the first century CE biographer Plutarch relates that Alexander needed 20,000 mules and 5,000 camels to carry it away—but what remains of the city today is both a reminder of the might of ancient Persia and of Alexander's incredible achievement in bringing it to its knees.

Begun under Darius I (ruled 522–486 BCE) and completed under his successors, Xerxes I (ruled 486–465 BCE) and Artaxerxes III (ruled 358–338 BCE), Persepolis was intended as both a fortress and a summer retreat where the court could escape the heat of Persia's other imperial cities, Babylon and Susa, in an area that would have provided rich hunting grounds. Raised on a terrace measuring 125,000 square meters

(1.35 million square feet), with its eastern end cut into the mountain, its crown was a palace of grey marble reached by a monumental staircase. From here, envoys bringing tribute from across the empire entered the great Hall of All Nations, passing a pair of statues of bulls with bearded men's heads known as "Lamussus" and through double doors that were probably covered in decorated sheets of metal. Supported by four imposing columns (which can still be seen), the hall measured 25 meters (82 feet) in length. Another majestic doorway led into a courtyard from where favored visitors could enter the Apadana. With a tower at each of its corners, this grand audience chamber—measuring 60 by 60 meters (200 by 200 feet)—was richly decorated with gold and tiled designs and signified the power and wealth of the Persian King of Kings. Seventy-two columns, each 19 meters (62 feet) tall and featuring a carved bull, supported a ceiling made from rare wood.

Even larger was the 70 by 70 meter (230 by 230 foot) Throne Hall (sometimes called the Hall of Honor or Hall of A Hundred Columns),

where the Persian kings once received military commanders and the most important nobles from across the realm. With its northern portico guarded by two massive stone bulls, the eight doorways were decorated with scenes of the king in combat with various mythical creatures. By the time Alexander the Great reached Persepolis, however, it was used as a museum, displaying the finest objets d'art and booty from the overflowing imperial treasury.

Elsewhere, the citadel contained everything necessary to cater to the needs of the great kings, including a harem, council chambers, stables, and storerooms, as well as the beautiful personal palace built

for Darius, which was surpassed only by the Palace of Xerxes. Known as the Hadish Palace, this was built at the highest level and would have served as his personal apartments. It featured balconies overlooking the surrounding landscape and a thirty-six-columned main hall with doorways leading off to guardrooms, a tower, and bedchambers. Sadly, little now remains of the palace, but the King of Kings would have demanded decoration that went far beyond mere extravagance.

The entire citadel was fortified by three walls, each studded with towers of increasing size. Any attacking enemy would first have to overwhelm a 2 meter (7 foot) wall only to be faced by another double

*Previous page, left:* Known as the Tachara, the palace of Darius I was incomplete at the time of the king's death in 486 BCE, but finished by his son, Xerxes.

*Previous page, right:* The Gate of All Nations, guarded by the *Lammussus*—bearded, human-headed bulls.

*Above:* From the Hall of All Nations (to the right of the photo), important visitors would approach the columned hall of the Apadana (left). Many of its columns are thought to have been carved from rare and precious woods that were burned when Alexander the Great torched Persepolis.

*Below, far left:* Persepolis has many exquisite bas-relief carvings, this one shows Armenians bringing the king of kings his tribute—their region's famous wine.

*Below left:* Reliefs and statues at Persepolis also feature beasts that were important in Persian mythology, such as this lion in combat with a bull.

*Below:* This bas-relief shows the Immortals, the empire's elite infantry force who also served as the king's formidable bodyguard.

*Left:* Columns in the Apadana and elsewhere around Persepolis were topped with carvings of animals, such as bulls, lions, and eagles as well as magnificent mythical beasts such as this griffin.

*Right:* The ruins of the Apadana with the Tachara Palace of Darius I in the distance.

its height. By this time exhausted, the attackers would finally meet a 9 meter (30 foot) wall, heavily manned by the empire's finest soldiers. Yet Alexander overcame all these obstacles and after making sacrifices to the gods ordered a celebratory feast. Otherwise known for treating his conquered enemies with respect (he often left them in post, demanding only obeisance) it is said that the Macedonian king and his commanders became drunk and decided that the destruction of such an exquisite citadel would provide a fitting revenge after

the ruin of Athens' acropolis at Persian hands 150 years earlier. After stripping the palace of most of its valuables (many fine works of art were reportedly lost), Alexander is supposed to have personally set the fire that gutted the fabulous buildings.

Subsequently, Persepolis all but disappeared from history. Although it was correctly identified as the site of Alexander's revenge as early as 1618, it wasn't until 1930 that a full-scale archaeological survey began. Today, the citadel lies in ruins but among its broken pillars remain reliefs and sculptures that speak of exquisite workmanship, fit for the kings of the greatest empire the world has seen.

### Site information:

| | |
|---|---|
| **Location:** | Fars Province, Iran |
| **Type of structure:** | Ancient Persian citadel |
| **Area:** | 25,000 square meters (1.35 million square feet) |
| **Completed:** | 515 BCE–330 CE |
| **Date of Inscription as a UNESCO World Heritage Site:** | 1979 |
| **UNESCO Criteria:** | (i) (iii) (vi) |

# EPHESUS
## TURKEY

*Now a part of modern Turkey, the ancient city of Ephesus has long been a counter in the games of kings and empires.*

ORIGINALLY SETTLED AROUND 6000 BCE, OVER THE COURSE OF ITS HISTORY Ephesus was colonized by the ancient Greeks, then conquered by the legendarily wealthy King Croesus, became a satrapy of the Persian Empire, was liberated by Alexander the Great, and then taken into the Roman Empire. Finally surrendering to the Turks in 1304, the city was abandoned during the fifteenth century. During this turbulent history, spanning 2,500 years from the time of the Greek settlers, it became one of the most illustrious cities on the Mediterranean Sea: a renowned hub of both trade and the arts, and consequently well endowed with some of the most incredible buildings erected anywhere in the ancient world.

Sadly, little now can be seen of the Temple of Artemis that was completed c. 550 BCE. Once the largest temple in existence (it was four times the size of the Parthenon in Athens) and one of the Seven Wonders of the Ancient World, only a few broken columns remain. Nevertheless, thanks to archaeological work that has been on-going since the nineteenth century, today's Ephesus boasts a fabulous wealth of ancient relics. Many of the city's best-preserved buildings date from the Roman period, indeed, it has been said that walking through the 210 meter (690 foot) length of the city's main street—Curetes Way—now is like walking through a Roman city without having to use any imagination to recreate the sights. Still in place are statues, shop fronts, latrines, and public buildings that the ancient citizens would have used daily—even carved stone "boards" for the popular game of *ludus duodecim scriptorum* (game of twelve markings).

Other sights include many fine works of architecture, appropriate to one of history's principal cities. One of the most popular with modern visitors is the elegant Library of Celsus. Built around 117 CE as a library and mausoleum for the Roman Senator Tiberius Julius Celsus Polemaeanus (c. 45–120 CE), the library once housed 12,000 scrolls, rivaling the great stores of knowledge in Rome and Alexandria. Designed by the celebrated architect Vitruoya, its interior hall was aligned east to provide light for those who preferred to work in the early morning and its exterior decorated with columns and niches for statues.

Built into the side of a hill with sweeping views over the stage in the Greek fashion, the Great Theater of Ephesus is a legacy of the love of the arts shown by the city's citizens. Mentioned in the Bible's Acts (Chapter 19) as the site of a riot provoked by the apostle Paul's preaching of the new religion, the theater dates to the third century BCE. Remodeled by the Romans, it was one of the largest of its kind in the ancient world with a capacity of 25,000.

Less monumental but equally interesting are the terraced Roman houses that stand opposite Hadrian's Temple (which honored the builder of Hadrian's Wall and is a superb expression of Roman architecture). These would have once been home to wealthy families and are in an excellent state of preservation. Beautifully designed, with mosaic floors and painted frescoes on the walls, as well as examples of the graffiti the Romans loved, these offer a vivid insight into the luxury of Roman life for its upper classes.

Elsewhere in Ephesus are two more great thoroughfares: Marble Street and Harbor Way. The older of the two is Marble Street, which dates to around the first century CE, leading from the Great Theater to the Temple of Artemis. Paved with marble, this was once part of the Sacred Way, but even here are signs of Roman exuberance—a discreet sign points the way to the nearest brothel. Stretching over half a kilometer (1,650 feet), Harbor Way was a later addition to the city and an attempt to revive its dwindling fortunes. Built during the reign of the

Byzantine Emperor Arcadius (ruled 395–408 CE), the street was one of the very few in the ancient world to be lit at night and was home to the most exclusive shops.

At the height of its glory, Ephesus was a significant maritime city where sailors brawled in the harbor bars while fortunes were made by international traders who then spent lavishly on their fabulous homes. Over the centuries, however, silt carried by the Cayster River clogged its port (which was moved a number of times to avoid the problem). Eventually, trade moved away completely and Ephesus slipped into history, but today the city has come alive again as a major tourist attraction and archaeological hub. Further digs at the site have been somewhat hampered by political events in recent times, but the uncovering of Ephesus' marvels continues.

*Previous page:* The Temple of Artemis in Ephesus was once the biggest in existence and one of the Seven Wonders of the Ancient World.

*Below left:* Curetes Way runs between Hercules Gate and the Celsus Library. It was lined on either side with statues, shops, and fountains.

*Right:* Detail of the elaborate stone carving at the Celsus Library give some idea of why the building is considered to be one of the great works of Roman architecture.

*Below:* The façade of the Celsus Library, which was the third largest library in the ancient world at the time when Ephesus was a Roman city. It housed over 12,000 scrolls.

*Above:* With capacity for 25,000 spectators, Ephesus's Great Theater was built into the side of a hill in the Greek style and later enlarged by Roman architects.

*Opposite page, left:* Now protected under cover, Ephesus's terrace houses offer an impression of the elegance the city's wealthier families would have enjoyed. On the right, the mosaic floor tiling depicts the snake-headed Medusa.

*Opposite page, right:* Built c. 138 CE, Hadrian's Temple on Curetes Way was dedicated to the Roman emperor who built Hadrian's Wall.

### Site information:

| | |
|---|---|
| **Location:** | Selçuk, Turkey |
| **Type of structure:** | Ancient Greek/Roman city |
| **Area:** | 4.15 square kilometers (1.6 square miles) |
| **Completed:** | Tenth century BCE–fifteenth century CE |
| **Date of Inscription as a UNESCO World Heritage Site:** | 2015 |
| **UNESCO Criteria:** | (iii) (iv) (vi) |

# HIERAPOLIS-PAMMUKALE
## TURKEY

*The relics of Roman-built bath towns can be found throughout the former empire but no other spa was quite as spectacular as ancient Hierapolis in the region known in classical times as Phrygia.*

BUILT OVER THERMAL SPRINGS AMID UNIQUE TERRACES OF NATURAL BASINS AND PETRIFIED WATERFALLS, Hierapolis rose within an alien, captivating landscape and attracted visitors from across the Mediterranean world. In fact, the mineral-rich springs here were believed to have curative properties as early as the second century BCE when the area was originally settled by Greeks. However, after Hierapolis was gifted to Rome by its last Greek ruler, Attalus III (170–133 BCE), it blossomed into a center of healing that was renowned around the empire. At its peak, the town had a permanent population of around 100,000, including a large number of Jews (many

of them doctors), as well as believers in the Greek and Roman deities, and Christians from Greece, Rome, and further afield—all of whom appeared to have lived in harmony for the most part. With its pleasant climate, peaceful atmosphere, luxurious baths, and many opportunities for diversion, the town was particularly attractive to wealthy retirees, though Hierapolis also held out the promise of cures to large numbers of travelers seeking help with medical conditions.

After being almost completely destroyed by an earthquake in 60 CE, much of the early Greek architecture was replaced by Roman buildings, the remains of which now stand testament to the town's former wealth and popularity. Bookended by imposing gates, Hierapolis' wide main street stretched over a 1,500 meters (4,900 feet) and was flanked on each side by covered arcades that provided protection from sun and rain to the town's citizens and visitors, as well as space for shops and restaurants. Any self-respecting Roman citizen would have demanded

*Below:* A spectacular view over the natural terraces and petrified formations that earned the site the name of Pammukale—meaning "Cotton Castle."

more from their town's public amenities though, and Hierapolis gave them everything they needed. Standing close to the northern gate a grand triumphal arch known as the Domitian Gate, which dates to around 85 CE, provided monumental architecture. Citizens could also spend their leisure time at a large theater, which had a capacity of 15,000 spectators, get fit at the gymnasium, or use an extensive library.

Hierapolis was closely associated with the gods (its name means "sacred city.") Indeed, its first building, which was destroyed by earthquakes, was a temple dated to around the 3rd century BCE. Its site was later occupied by the once-spectacular Temple of Apollo, which featured a huge fountain that supplied the domestic water needs for the town, as well as a passage that led to a subterranean cave known as the "Gate of Hell." As at Delphi, noxious fumes seeping from the ground here were said to inspire oracular prophecies, which could be purchased for a fee. Dedicated to the gods of the Underworld, so thick with gases was the cave that small birds and animals died upon entering.

It was Hierapolis' baths that secured the town's prosperity though, and the town had no fewer than fifteen—constructed from huge travertine blocks—allowing hundreds of people to take the waters at any one time, within elegant, columned surroundings. With the temperature ranging between 36–57 °C (97–135 °F), the water contains a combination of minerals including bicarbonate, iron, and sulphate. It was used for drinking cures and for the long, leisurely soaks that remain popular with today's visitors. The water's healing properties were said to be particularly efficacious for ailments such as arthritis, skin diseases, and abdominal distress.

The waters didn't always provide the cures people were seeking, however. The town has an unusually large necropolis containing graves and tombs that date back to the early Greek occupation. Hierapolis' most famous tomb though is the Martyrium. The church, which dates to the fifth century CE, stands just outside the city walls and is reputed to have been built over the grave of St. Philip (though there is some

*Left:* To the north of Hierapolis are the two towers (one of which can be seen to the left of this photograph) and the three massive stone block arches of the Domitian Gate.

dispute about this). The apostle of Christ is thought to have been one of the few casualties of religious tension in Hierapolis—he was crucified upside down after preaching against other deities.

Abandoned in the fourteenth century CE after a series of earthquakes, international attention returned to Hierapolis after an archaeological dig uncovered the town in the late nineteenth century. By the early twentieth century, it was—again—a popular tourist attraction, named Pamukkale (Cotton Castle) for its dazzling white mineral formations and deposits.

Today, the ancient town preserves the refined atmosphere of a venerable spa where the sick came to be healed and the rich came to spend their final years in comfort.

*Right:* Hierapolis was principally a health resort and spa town boasting fifteen baths. Today, these contain fragments of the town's past but are still used by modern visitors.

*Left:* Hierapolis's theater—like that of Ephesus—was enlarged from an original structure by the Romans to contain up to 15,000 customers at a seating. It offered drama and spectacle, as well as sweeping views over the landscape.

*Below left:* The St. Philip Martyrium stands on a hill to the northeast of the city.

| Site information: | |
|---|---|
| **Location:** | Pamukkale, Turkey |
| **Type of structure:** | Ancient Greek/Roman spa town |
| **Area:** | 10 square kilometers (4 square miles) |
| **Completed:** | Second century BCE–fourteenth century CE |
| **Date of Inscription as a UNESCO World Heritage Site: 1988** | |
| **UNESCO Criteria:** | (iii) (iv) (vii) |

# ANGKOR WAT
## CAMBODIA

*Standing at the heart of the Angkor Archaeological Park, the huge Angkor Wat temple complex is the symbolic heart of Cambodia itself.*

ONCE THOUGHT TO HAVE BEEN SIMPLY A VAST COLLECTION OF NEIGHBORING TEMPLES, recent high-tech aerial studies have shown that Angkor Wat was actually the hub of a sprawling conurbation that stretched for tens of kilometers and which would have comprised the largest city on Earth until the time of the Industrial Revolution.

Angkor Wat itself is a stupendous work of architecture, superbly designed with an eye for proportion and harmony, and encompassing myth and mysteries within its design. Originally dedicated to the god Vishnu, fables tell that it was built by divine hands over the course of a single night though, in fact, it was constructed over decades during the reign of the Khmer king, Suryavarman II (ruled 1113–50 CE), and served as the Hindu state temple until it became a Buddhist temple the following century. Because Angkor Wat's builders oriented the temple towards the west—associated with Vishnu and death in Hinduism—it is believed that it may have been intended as the king's mausoleum, though it was never used for that purpose.

Occupying a site of 400 square kilometers (155 square miles), and surrounded by a wide moat and forested area where the royal palace and official buildings once stood, the main temple rises from a terrace in a series of three galleries within an enclosing wall. The second-level gallery features a tower at each corner, dominated by a central tower that stands 65 meters (213 feet) tall. The layout is rich in symbolism. The entire site is said to represent the universe with the central tower as Mount Meru, the home of the gods. The tower itself is approached by an extremely steep staircase (reaching the home of the gods should be no easy stroll, after all) that was once guarded at the top by a statue of Vishnu. At the time of construction, this area would have been forbidden to all but a select few. As Eleanor Mannikka describes in her book, *Angkor: Celestial Temples of the Khmer Empire*, it was the center of the Khmer nation—a place where the king and divine forces came together and therefore the most sacred part of the empire.

Architecturally, the building is in the Khmer style; its towers are reminiscent of lotus buds and it is richly endowed with decoration, including the incredible bas relief—the largest of its kind—that depicts Samudra manthan, the Hindu creation myth. Here *devas* (gods) and *asuras* (demons) work together under Vishnu's guidance to churn the "sea of milk" to produce the elixir of immortality. In fact, almost the entire surface of the temple, including its roof, is covered with reliefs. Depicted in carved stone are mythical creatures, battles, royal processions, significant religious scenes, images of the Naga (the snake king who protected the empire), and around 1,850 female spirits and nymphs—so many that the temple has been described as a shrine to the feminine. It is said that each of these was carved

*Previous page:* Angkor Wat reflected in one of the two pools located in the temple grounds. At the heart of the largest religious site anywhere in the world, it was originally built as a Hindu temple but had become a Buddhist site by the end of the twelfth century CE.

*Left:* The five towers of Angkor Wat form an arrangement known as a "quincunx" and represent the five peaks of Mount Meru, the home of the gods.

as a portrait of one of Suryavarman's many wives, concubines, and favorite dancing girls.

As might be expected of such a fabulously ornate and intensely spiritual site, Angkor Wat has inspired many people to imagine great secrets woven into its design. To many its sheer size and complexity seem an impossibility, well beyond the skill of the builders of the time. Many Cambodians still believe that prophecies of the future are carved into its walls, while unconventional theorist Graham Hancock proposes that there is evidence at the site to support his idea of a lost civilization attempting to preserve its knowledge through buildings that mirror the stars. He argues that the area's temples represent the constellation Draco as it would have appeared 10,500 years ago, in the same way that the Giza pyramids represented Orion. Eleanor Mannikka, too, has found astronomical features in the temple's design that suggest it may have been intended as more than a simple place of worship. Mysteries aside, Suryavarman II ruled during a golden age of the Khmer Empire and— had a vast workforce at his disposal. It is thought that around 300,000 people would have been involved in the construction, floating the stone blocks used in its construction 40 kilometers (25 miles) along canals from a quarry to the north and placing them with the utmost precision. The nation's finest architects and stone carvers would also have been conscripted into the building of such an important monument.

Unusually among the ancient monuments in this book, Angkor Wat has remained in continuous use since it was built, though it has not escaped the passage of centuries unmarked. Art robbers have stolen many statues, while botched restoration and encroaching vegetation have also taken their toll. Nevertheless, Angkor Wat has never been

*Above:* The interior walls of Angkor Wat's main temple and its corridors are as intricately carved as the exterior.

*Below:* Angkor Wat is still a place of Buddhist pilgrimage.

plundered for its stone, like so many other amazing sites, and it remains in comparatively excellent shape. Today, it is a site of enormous national pride for the Cambodian people, so much so that it is depicted on their flag. It is now rigorously protected and intensively studied. As our knowledge of the temple and its surroundings grows, so, too, does human interest. As recently as the early 1990s, Angkor Wat received just a few thousand visitors each year. Now that number exceeds two million annually.

*Above:* Detail from the relief that depicts "the churning of the sea of milk," the largest continuous bas-relief in the world.

*Above left:* Angkor Wat's many carvings cover subjects as serious as creation and war, as well as much lighter scenes such as these beautifully realized dancing girls.

*Opposite page, above:* There are also many carvings of apsaras. Equivalent to European nymphs, apsaras were female supernatural beings who excelled at singing and dancing.

*Opposite page, below:* Carving and paintings around the temple also depict important scenes from the life of King Suryavarman II.

**Site information:**

| | |
|---|---|
| **Location:** | Siem Reap Province, Cambodia |
| **Type of structure:** | Temple Complex |
| **Length (outer wall):** | 1,025 meters (3,360 feet) |
| **Width (outer wall):** | 800 meters (2,625 feet) |
| **Height (central tower):** | 65 meters 9213 feet) |
| **Completed:** | c. 1113–1150 |
| **Date of Inscription as a UNESCO World Heritage Site:** | 1992 |
| **UNESCO Criteria:** | (i) (ii) (iii) (iv) |

# THE GREAT WALL
## CHINA

*The largest military defense ever built, the Great Wall of China stretches 21,196 kilometers (13,171 miles) in its entirety, from the Jiayuguan Pass at its western extremity to Bohai Gulf in the east.*

SNAKING ACROSS MOUNTAINS, PLAINS, AND DESERTS ALONG ITS ROUTE, THE GREAT WALL OF CHINA cost the lives of hundreds of thousands to build. But for centuries it protected the Chinese Empire from the mounted hordes of Mongolia, while also serving to regulate trade along the famous Silk Road. Commonly believed to be a single, uninterrupted edifice, the Great Wall in fact comprises a number of structures: some branching from the main length of the wall, others abandoned as the empire grew or shrank and left completely isolated. Its builders also took advantage of natural defensive features such as mountains in the landscape, breaking its length. Another misconception is that the wall is the only human construction that can be seen from space. While this notion gives some sense of the wall's incredible size, it is, disappointingly, untrue.

Wall-building as a defensive strategy dates back to China's pre-imperial past: as long ago as the eighth century BCE. At that time, the separate states that would become China under Qin Shi Huang (meaning Qin, the First Emperor) built their own simple walls of earth and stones to guard their borders. After successfully uniting his new empire in 221 BCE, the first emperor ordered these demolished, save those sections that could be incorporated into a new wall that would protect the empire's northern border. Over the following fourteen centuries, a succession of rulers repaired, enlarged, and extended these walls, usually relying on local materials for the construction. For this reason little remains of long sections where the wall was made from easily-eroded rammed earth.

The fourteenth century brought renewed military pressure from the Mongolian tribes, and in response the Ming rulers began a fresh period of wall repair and new building. This time, they used stone and brick. Due to the sturdy and relatively recent construction, the Ming sections have weathered the passage of time better than other areas of the wall and now provide the popular conception of the Great Wall of China.

Beginning during the reign of Emperor Yongle (ruled 1402–24), building by the Ming reached a peak in the mid-sixteenth century and continued until the dynasty fell in 1644. Studded with around 25,000 watchtowers, as well as fortified gates, the Ming walls stretch 8,850 kilometers (5,500 miles) and are 5–8 meters tall (16–26 feet) with a width at the base of around 6 meters (20 feet) tapering to 5 meters (16 feet) at the top. Completed with a rampart-protected "street" upon which soldiers could move quickly to wherever they were needed, the work was a massive undertaking requiring a correspondingly massive workforce. Forced labor was common. At its peak, it is said that one in every three Chinese males was involved in the building: transporting stone, working in the huge kilns where bricks were fired, or mortaring endless bricks into place. Some estimates put the number of lives spent during construction at well over a million, of which many were

convicted criminals who were worked to death. It has been reported that if one man died before his sentence was complete a family member would be dragged to the wall to replace him. Such a vast and painful national effort sparked widespread national protests and was reflected in the work of poets. One wrote:

> *Every brick, every stone,*
> *and every inch of mud*
> *are filled with Chinese people's*
> *bones and sweat and blood.*

The result of all this backbreaking toil was a structure that eventually failed to perform its intended task. In 1644, general Wu Sangui (1612–78) opened the gates to Manchu forces at Shanhai Pass, bringing an end to the Ming dynasty. Even so, the wall stands as an enduring monument to the people who built it. Widely recognized as one of the New Seven Wonders of the World, the Great Wall of China is one of the nation's most visited tourist attractions and features numerous significant points along its great length. One of the most popular with modern visitors is at Jinshanling, about 125 kilometers

*Previous spread:* A superb sunrise view of a Ming Dynasty section of the wall near Beijing.

*Right:* A statue of the Yongle Emperor who was responsible for beginning the massive wall-building program of the Ming Dynasty.

*Below:* Jiayuguan Pass at the western end of the Great Wall was one of the most important entry points into China and is now one of the best preserved fortresses along its length.

(77 miles) northeast of Beijing. Dating to around 1570, the section winds through the spectacular mountainous landscape here.

Elsewhere, at the western end of the wall, stands the fortress gate of Jiayuguan Pass. Less visited than the more accessible and scenic sections of China's Great Wall, the pass was once an important waypoint on the Silk Road and is associated with a revealing legend.

The story tells of Yi Kaizhan—a worker who had been a mathematician before being conscripted to work on the wall. Asked by the supervisor how many bricks would be required, Yi Kaizhan answered with an exact number: 99,999. Considering this

*Left*: A Ming Dynasty section of the wall at Jiayuguan, Gansu Province. Unlike other sections, this part of the wall was built of rammed earth and blends harmoniously with the desert landscape.

*Far left, below*: Traditionally, the Great Wall starts far to the east of Jiayuguan at Shanhaiguan (also known as the First Pass Under Heaven) in Qinhuangdao Prefecture, but it actually enters the ocean a little further down the road at a place called Old Dragon's Head.

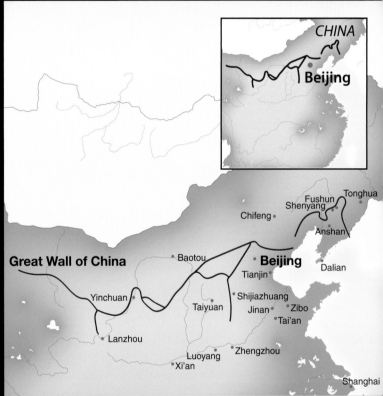

insubordinate, the supervisor told him that if he was incorrect by even one brick every man would be given an additional three years forced labor. When the fortress had been finished one brick remained unused on top of the gate. Seizing on this opportunity to wring an extra three years from his workforce, the supervisor reminded Yi Kaizhan of the punishment, to which the mathematician replied that the extra brick had been placed there by a spirit. If it were ever moved the fortress would collapse. The workers escaped their punishment and the brick remains in place to this day.

### Site information:

| | |
|---|---|
| Location: | China |
| Type of structure: | Fortification |
| Length: | 21,196 kilometers (13,171 miles) |
| Height: | 5–8 meters (16–26 feet) |
| Width (base): | 6 meters (20 feet) |
| Width (top): | 5 meters (16 feet) |
| Completed: | Third century BCE–1644 |

Date of Inscription as a UNESCO World Heritage Site: 1992

UNESCO Criteria: (i) (ii) (iii) (iv) (vi)

# HAMPI MONUMENTS
## INDIA

*Founded in 1336 by brothers Harihara I and Bukka Raya I, the empire of Vijayanagara once covered
a vast swathe of southern India.*

UNITED BY THE HINDU RELIGION AND RULED BY SUCCESSIVE DYNASTIES THAT ENCOURAGED TRADE AND INNOVATION, Hampi became a place of extraordinary wealth matched only by the flamboyant creativity of its arts and architecture. All of these came together at its capital, a place where precious gems are said to have been traded on street corners, and where the temples and royal palaces left early European travelers breathless with wonder. Following a heavy defeat by combined Muslim forces in 1565 the Vijayanagara Empire staggered heavily, then finally fell for good eighty years later, but at Hampi its people left behind a huge collection of amazing monuments amid a vivid green landscape of palm trees and lush vegetation.

Set in a river valley and protected by hills as well as a series of seven fortified walls, Hampi's architectural marvels comprise a list that would require a much bigger book to explore in detail. Strewn across an area of 26 square kilometers (10 square miles), they include impressive works of civil engineering such as a sophisticated aqueduct system, as well as large stone statues of deities, abandoned bazaars, riverside pavilions, defensive forts, numerous Hindi and Jain shrines and temples, streets wide enough to accommodate the vast imperial army, royal buildings including a stable for the king's elephants, and even a monumental scale where the ruler once weighed himself each year before donating his weight in gold and precious gems to the temples. At Hampi, everywhere the eye rests it finds ornate carvings to rival anything created by Greek or Roman sculptors.

One of the most impressive structures is the still largely intact Virupaksha Temple, which predates the Vijayanagara Empire and

*Above:* A panoramic photograph of the Vitthala Temple. In the left foreground is a shrine built in the form of a chariot, while the main temple is behind in the center of the shot.

*Below left:* The breathtaking carving of the Vitthala Temple demonstrates creativity and technical skill unmatched anywhere else at the Hampi site.

*Below:* This masterpiece of architecture was built to house Hampi's royal elephants. Each of the eleven domed chambers within would once have been home to two elephants.

remains in use today. Dating to around the seventh century CE, the temple was massively enlarged under its later rulers, who added features including a magnificently carved and colonnaded central hall and two imposing gateways. The distinctive nine-tiers of its eastern gate (built in 1442) have become an iconic symbol of Indian architecture, rising 50 meters (164 feet) in a semi-domed shape.

Even more famous is the Vitthala Temple. Dedicated to Lord Vitthala, an aspect of Lord Vishnu (the principal god in the Hindu pantheon), it is widely regarded as one of the planet's greatest works of architecture. Set in a large, walled and gated compound, the temple is surrounded by stunning pavilions and shrines (including one ingenious example that has been created in the form of a chariot and which once had turning wheels). None, however, manages to outshine the temple itself. With almost every inch decorated with exquisite carvings of animals, birds, flowers, and soldiers, its ornate roof is held aloft by pillars carved to represent musical instruments and which play notes when tapped (although visitors are forbidden to play tunes on them).

The royal buildings, too, demonstrate the incredible skill and creative dexterity of the Vijayanagara craftsmen. The compound comprises a number of buildings that would have housed the emperor

*Left:* The stunning Virupaksha Temple dates to the seventh century CE and was enlarged over the following centuries.

*Below:* Hidden behind a relatively plain exterior, the Queen's Bath is a beautifully ornate structure showing Islamic influences. It is likely that the bath was part of a pleasure complex used by the king as well as his queens.

and his queen along with functionaries and the royal court. It is at least as impressive as its European counterpart at Versailles (by way of contrast the population of Hampi at its peak was around half a million, three times that of Paris at the time). With the Hazara Rama temple at its heart, covered with some of the most beautiful and extensive reliefs found anywhere in Indian art, the Royal Center also boasts an elevated platform from which the king could observe religious festivals as well as a stunningly elegant bathing pool known as the Queen's Bath.

Nearby is the Lotus Mahal, a fanciful pavilion that shows Islamic influence in its design and which was probably used as a council chamber. The emperor's wealth also stretched to creating what must be the world's most unusual and handsome stable. Built to house his elephants, the building could easily have served a lesser king as a palace. Flanking a central, two-tiered tower, domes of alternating design rise above grand archways that lead into the elephants' stalls. Before the stable is a wide area that may have been a parade ground or exercise area for the animals.

While parts of Hampi were severely damaged during the Battle of Talikota (1565), which heralded its decline and eventual downfall, the city was "discovered" by the first British Surveyor General of India, Colonel Colin Mackenzie (1754–1821). Since then it has delighted generations of visitors—some of whom may be lucky enough to receive the blessing of a temple elephant in the form of a "kiss." Today, its past continues to be revealed by archaeologists and researchers working for numerous organizations while the city's magnificent gateways lead tourists into an astounding period of Indian imperial history.

*Above:* One of the most distinctive structures at Hampi is the Lotus Mahal. As its name suggests, it was designed to recall the shape of a lotus bud rising from its leaf just before opening.

*Right:* A view through the symmetrical arches on the ground floor of the Lotus Mahal. The floor above features beautiful windowed balconies while evidence of the building's original "air conditioning" can be found in the surviving pipework.

### Site information:

**Location:**         Karnataka Bellary District, India

**Type of structure:**   Capital city of the Vijayanagara Empire

**Area:**             26 square kilometers (10 square miles)

**Completed:**        1336–1565

**Date of Inscription as a UNESCO World Heritage Site:** 1986—minor modification inscribed year: 2012

**UNESCO Criteria:**    (i) (iii) (iv)

# BOROBUDUR TEMPLE
## INDONESIA

*The massive temple was hidden beneath thick volcanic ash and deep jungle for hundreds of years until it was rediscovered by the outside world in the early nineteenth century.*

IN BUDDHIST TRADITION A MANDALA IS A GEOMETRIC PATTERN OF A SQUARE WITH FOUR ENTRY POINTS containing further squares areound a central circle. Said to represent the cosmos, a mandala is used for religious guidance. The largest ever made—and the largest Buddhist monument anywhere—stands on the Indonesian island of Java. The colossal structure, which resembles a giant pyramid and contains over two million stone blocks, serves as both a shrine and a spiritual lesson. Rising in ever smaller platforms from a square base that measures 118 meters (387 feet) on each side, the series of platforms— six square and three circular—provides pilgrims with an instructional journey of over 3 kilometers (2 miles), featuring 2,672 panels of carved reliefs interspersed with 504 Buddha statues.

Following the route through the monument, pilgrims climb up stairs and beneath gateways through successive levels of understanding towards enlightenment and Nirvana. Although no written records exist of its construction, archaeological studies of Borobudur place its

construction date to about 825 CE, during the reign of the Javan king Samaratungga (ruled c. 812–33). Built without mortar, it is thought the monument took around seventy-five years to complete and it was embellished with carvings of lions and everyday scenes, along with reliefs that offer spiritual messages. Around two centuries after it was finished Borobudur was abandoned when the eruption of nearby Mount Merapi covered it with a thick layer of volcanic ash—an event that may have caused a famine, forcing the local inhabitants to migrate. For

*Right:* One of Borobudur's Buddha statues, seated in the lotus position. The temple originally had 504 Buddhas, but forty-three are now missing, while 300 have been damaged.

*Far right:* The site also features numerous lion statues that stand guard at gates.

*Below:* A panorama of Borobudur taken from the northwest. The platform encasing the original lowest level can be seen at the monument's base.

centuries, the great structure lay obscured beneath its thick blanket until the British lieutenant-governor Sir Thomas Stamford Raffles (1781–1826) learned of its whereabouts in 1812. Curious, Raffles sent a party to unearth whatever was beneath the mound that had, by that time, been reclaimed by the jungle. The team of 200 men revealed the vast edifice to the world once again. By 1835, the entire site was uncovered and over the following decades, Borobudur captured the world's imagination, as well as the attention of art thieves who plundered many of the temple's statues. The Javan governors also helped themselves, notably gifting many sculptures to the king of Siam during an 1896 state visit.

Today, Borobudur is Indonesia's most popular attraction, visited by millions of tourists and pilgrims each year. To the latter it still provides religious instruction. Often likened to a gigantic stone textbook, paths

and stairways lead the pilgrim through a circumambulatory, ever-ascending journey. The lowest levels represent Kamadhatu, the worldly realm of human desire, though the very bottom level is thought to have been encased during construction, possibly due to catastrophic subsidence which meant that the structure had to be buttressed. Another theory suggests that the original layer may have been incorrectly built. Whatever the cause, the original carvings—depicting the baseness of human nature with scenes of robbery, murder, and rape—were covered. Rediscovered in 1885, a portion of the original scenes are now again revealed to visitors.

From the realm of Kamadhatu, the aspiring pilgrim ascends to Rapadhatu, where humans remain chained to physical form but have cast off worldly concerns and desires. These four, square levels are lined with niches containing statues of Buddha as well as reliefs and texts that

recount Prince Siddhartha's progress from cossetted childhood through his long and painful search for wisdom before he eventually reached enlightenment and manifestation as Buddha.

At the highest levels, the structure changes from a square layout to the final circular stages, representing Arupadhatu, the realm of the gods. Surrounded by seventy-two magnificent, bell-like stupas (many of which contain statues of the kneeling Buddha that can be seen through decorative "windows") this is the sphere of "formlessness" where physical names and forms are finally cast off. Here, there are no further reliefs or carved instructions. The circular form symbolizes the endless cycles of eternity and the serene state of spiritual eternity. The peak of Borobudur is crowned with a colossal stupa, which reaches 35 meters (115 feet) above ground level. The building is monumental in every sense of the word.

*Above:* Borobudur has 2,670 bas-reliefs, of which 1,212 are decorative. The rest offer spiritual tutelage and guidance, showing the life (and former lives) of the Buddha.

Happily, during the twentieth century the site benefitted from several restoration projects including a major UNESCO-led effort between 1975 and 1982. It was designated a World Heritage Site in 1991 along with two other Buddhist temples in the same region—Pawon and Mendut. Together, the three temples describe a straight line—for reasons that remain unclear. Despite the loss of many of its stone treasures, Borobudur retains its atmosphere of reflective tranquillity. More than a thousand years after being built, it continues to serve the purpose for which it was intended.

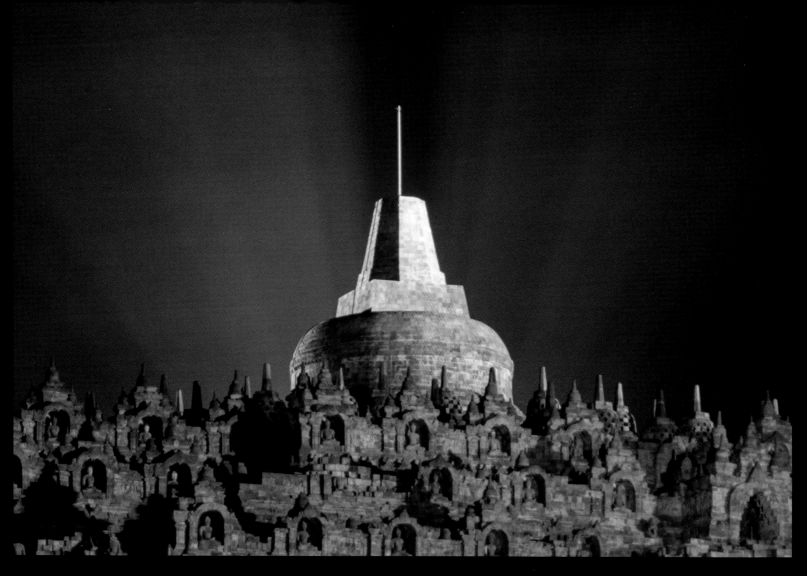

*Above:* The huge central stupa that crowns Borobudur illuminated at night.

*Opposite page:* An evocative photograph taken at dawn through the large, bell-shaped stupas that surround Borobudur's summit. All but the largest contain seated Buddhas, which can be viewed through the decorative holes.

| Site information: | |
|---|---|
| Location: | Regency of Magelang, Province of Central Java, Indonesia |
| Type of structure: | Temple |
| Length: | 118 meters (387 feet) |
| Width: | 118 meters (387 feet) |
| Height: | 35 meters (115 feet) |
| Completed: | c: 750–825 CE |
| Date of Inscription as a UNESCO World Heritage Site: | 1991 |
| UNESCO Criteria: | (i) (ii) (vi) |

# BAGAN
## MYANMAR

*The Myanmar city of Bagan was built by a royal dynasty that has long since disappeared but which left an astonishing architectural legacy of 10,000 breathtaking temples, shrines, pagodas, and monasteries.*

TODAY, ABOUT A FIFTH OF THE ORIGINAL BUILDINGS STILL STAND—ABOUT 8,000 HAVE BEEN LOST TO EARTHQUAKES AND THE PASSAGE OF TIME—but those that remain dot the landscape for miles like shining islands rising from a sea of green.

From the ninth century CE to the thirteenth century, Bagan was the heart of the Pagan Kingdom, which unified the country that would later become Burma under one ruler for the first time, and laid the foundations for Burmese language and civilization. Under a succession of (mostly) shrewd kings, the country experienced

a "golden age" for about two hundred years, starting from the beginning of the eleventh century. Untroubled by any serious outbreaks of war, Pagan took strands of culture from its neighbors (notably India) and wove them into a distinctive culture of its own. As the kingdom expanded and new irrigation systems increased revenues, the country's newfound riches were lavished on its capital. Bagan became a renowned center of the arts, learning, and religion and a site of Buddhist pilgrimage with its glittering golden domes and pinnacles spread across 104 square kilometers (40 square miles) over the Irrawaddy river plains. Typically domed and topped

with a point or spire known as a hti, the stupa design originated in India. Temples of this type usually held sacred relics or were used as mausoleums. The Gu-style temples developed closer to home in city states that later came under Pagan dominion, although the native Mon style was fused with Indian influences. Usually based on a square pattern, often with projecting entrances, the style is characterized by stepped rooflines—again crowned with hti. Temples of this type were generally used for meditation, worship, and rituals.

Of the latter type, Bagan's largest example is the dominating, pyramid-shaped, Dhammayangyi Temple. Measuring 78 meters (255 feet) on each side at its base, the temple was built during the short reign of one of the kingdom's less enlightened kings: Narathu (ruled 1167–70). Having claimed the throne after murdering his father and brother (he is also said to have executed his Indian wife for refusing to give up Hinduism), legend tells that Narathu built the vast edifice to

expiate his sin. In spite of this, he inflicted dreadful punishments during its construction, chopping the arms off anyone whose work failed to meet his exacting standards. After his assassination in 1170, the temple was largely filled with bricks; possibly as a measure to help it withstand earthquakes, though many believe this was "revenge" against the unlamented Narathu.

Ananda Pahto Temple is stylistically similar, yet lighter and more graceful although one of the earliest to be built. Raised during the more enlightened rule of King Kyansittha (ruled 1084–1112), it is widely regarded as the Bagan's finest, and contains wonderful decorative carvings as well as four beautiful Buddhas carved from teak and covered in gold, each facing a different direction. Four projecting entrance halls give the temple a cruciform plan while six stepped terraces are crowned with a golden hti soaring 51 meters (167 feet) above the ground.

Unique among Bagan's relics, the Mahabodhi Temple was named

after the structure that inspired it (the original is in Bodhgaya, India). A steep-sided pyramid rising 43 meters (140 feet), it is similar to a number of other temples in the area though no other displays such a wealth of ornamentation. Niches in the tower, as well as in corner stupas are home to 450 Buddha statues.

These three examples are among the most celebrated in the city, but Bagan contains hundreds more beautiful buildings and shrines including golden pagodas such as fabulous Shwezigon Pagoda and the Lawkananda Pagoda. Dating to 1059, and the reign of the kingdom's founder—King Anawrahta (ruled 1044–77)—the pagoda once contained the tooth of the Gautama Buddha (it has now been replaced with a replica).

The Pagan Empire collapsed in the late thirteenth century after repeated Mongol invasions. Bagan itself survived the centuries as a site of pilgrimage, though its population never again reached the peaks of its golden era. The majority of its temples fell out of use and were neglected, while many more temples were destroyed by earthquakes. Now growing in popularity with visitors, Bagan has also been badly affected by political turbulence that in turn deterred tourism. Meanwhile, military governments repaired and restored some of the temples using modern techniques and materials. For this reason

*Previous pages:* Temples rise above the trees at Bagan. The largest, at the center of the image, is the Sulamani Temple, built in 1183 CE by King Narapatisithu.

*Above:* The four gold-leaf covered Buddhas of the Ananda Temple. Each faces a different direction and has a different name. From left to right: Gautama facing west; Konagamana, facing east; Kassapa facing south; and Kakusandha facing north.

UNESCO has been slow to adopt Bagan as a World Heritage Site. As the country settles into democracy and new efforts are made to preserve and restore Bagan's wonderful buildings in a sympathetic manner, it is hoped that this situation will soon be rectified and that the magnificent and ancient city will attract the attention it deserves on the world stage.

*Left:* Unique among the temples of Bagan, the design of the Mahabodhi Temple was inspired by that of the Mahabodhi Temple in Bihar, India.

*Below:* Niches in the Mahabodhi Temple contain 450 Buddha statues.

*Bottom:* This panoramic photograph shows just a few of the 2,200 temples that dot the landscape at Bagan. At its peak the site would have boasted around 10,000 assorted temples.

*Opposite page:* The stunning Shwezigon Pagoda. The crowning stupa is covered in gold-leaf, while the lower levels were cased in copper plates during a recent renovation. The structure was originally completed in 1102 CE.

**Site information:**

**Location:**  Mandalay Region, Myanamar

**Type of structure:**  Ancient City

**Area:**  1104 square kilometers (40 square miles)

**Completed:**  Ninth to thirteenth centuries CE

**Date of Inscription as a UNESCO World Heritage Site:** Submitted by Myanmar to the UNESCO "tentative list" in 1996

**UNESCO Criteria:**  (i) (ii) (iii) (iv) (v) (vi)

# AMERICAS

# GREAT SERPENT MOUND
## OHIO, USA

*From the Biblical tale of Adam and Eve in the Garden of Eden to the Rainbow Snake creator god of the Australian Aboriginal peoples, serpents appear with bewildering frequency in myths and folktales around the globe.*

OF ALL THE MYTHICAL SERPENTS OR SERPENT GODS AND IMAGES OF FABLED SNAKES CARVED INTO STONE none are as large as the Great Serpent Mound in Ohio, and none present such an inpenetrable mystery.

Built on a natural plateau and following the folds of the terrain, the mound measures 411 meters (1,348 feet), rising to a maximum height of about 1 meter (3 feet). Like the Nazca Lines its scale can only be truly appreciated from the air. At the western end, the snake's tail forms a spiral coil, then the body undulates eastward across the plateau in a slight crescent, ending in a stylized head. The gaping mouth appears about to consume an egg-shaped object. The structure was built using clay and ash, reinforced with stones.

That is about as much as can be said for certain about the mound. Almost everything else about it is hotly contested—even the date of its construction. Carbon dating of charcoal fragments found within its coils has proved inconclusive, providing dates that differ wildly between 300 BCE and 1070 CE; periods when two different cultures occupied

he territory and neither of which left any written records. The mound s commonly associated with the Adena Culture that lived in the region etween c. 1000 BCE and 100 CE, for the simple reason that the Adena eople are known mound builders. However, the Fort Ancient people, ho lived here between 1000 and 1750 CE, revered snakes and it is hought possible that if they didn't build the mound themselves, they nay have renovated it for their own mysterious purposes.

Why the enormous serpent was built is also the subject of debate. ike many other ancient monuments, the Great Snake Mound appears o mark the solstices and equinoxes, with its head facing the summer olstice sunset, and coils marking out other astronomical events. This uggests that it may have been used as a calendar. However, plenty of ther theories abound. Some believe that the egg-shape may represent he sun: so, like Apep the serpent god of Egyptian mythology, this erpent, too, may be a sun-eater. Others think it may represent Halley's Comet or some other great heavenly event such as a supernova; till others that—like Angkor Wat—it mirrors the pattern of the constellation Draco. Archaeologists familiar with the rites of the Adena olk suggest that it was used in funeral rites, directing the souls of the lead towards the spirit realm. Headless skeletons, fire-blackened stones, nd ceremonial knives discovered nearby might mean that the site was nce used for human sacrifice.

Frustratingly, it seems unlikely that the Great Serpent Mound's ourpose will ever be conclusively proved. Like other sites in this book t serves as a reminder that for all our technical wizardry much of our wn history remains cloaked in mystery.

*Top and Above:* The undulating body of the serpent rises between c. 30 centimetres–1 meter (1–3 feet) above ground level. No one knows for certain who built the mound but many archaeologists believe that it may have had astronomical significance.

*Opposite page:* This image shows the complete length of the snake from its coiled tail, slightly to the left at the center of the photograph, to its open mouth, ready to consume an egg-shaped object at the top. In total, the mound measures 411 meters (1,348 feet).

### Site information:

| | |
|---|---|
| **Location:** | Ohio, United States of America |
| **Type of structure:** | Ancient earthwork |
| **Length:** | 411 meters (1,348 feet) |
| **Height:** | 30 centimeters–1 meter (1–3 feet) |
| **Completed:** | Inconclusive |

**Date of Inscription as a UNESCO World Heritage Site:** Submitted by United States of America to the UNESCO "tentative list" in 2008

**UNESCO Criteria:** (i) (iii) (iv)

# NAZCA LINES
## PERU

*In the remote, arid plains of the Nazca desert in southern Peru, more than 400 kilometers (250 miles) southeast of Lima, lies a centuries-old mystery literally etched into the land.*

IMPOSSIBLE TO FULLY COMPREHEND FROM GROUND LEVEL, THE NAZCA LINES COVER MORE THAN 450 SQUARE KILOMETERS (175 SQUARE MILES) of desert and comprise over 800 straight lines with 300 geometric shapes, and 70 plant and animal figures, including monkeys, birds, spiders, and humans. The geoglyph figures range from 15 to 367 meters (50–1,200 feet) in length—longer than the height of the Empire State Building.

Dating from between c. 500 BCE and 500 CE, the question of how the Nazca Lines were made is no longer the subject of great debate. Similar markings have been produced by small teams working with the same sort of surveying tools that would have been available to the original artists. Having plotted their images, the Nazca folk simply removed the reddish-brown gravelly surface of the desert to reveal the lighter clay soil that lies about 15 centimeters (6 inches) beneath. Arid conditions in the desert have done an excellent job of preserving them in an almost pristine state over the subsequent centuries.

Why they were made is a more controversial subject and has provoked numerous theories, including one made by the best-selling author Erich von Däniken in the late 1960s. Famously, von Däniken proposed that the lines were used as landing markers for alien spacecraft. Unsurprisingly, that theory has been widely debunked. Others have suggested that the giant images were etched in the desert to be viewed from above, by the Nazca gods, or that they might have been used as processional ways for religious rites. One of the most convincing theories is that proposed by Paul Kosok (1896–1959) who originally recognized the significance of the lines—when flying over the desert in 1941 he noticed the shape of a hummingbird scratched from the surface of the desert. Kosok believed that the Nazca Lines, like so many other ancient monuments, were used as celestial markers—charting solstices and mapping star positions on the ground. Other experts in the field maintain that the evidence for this is inconclusive.

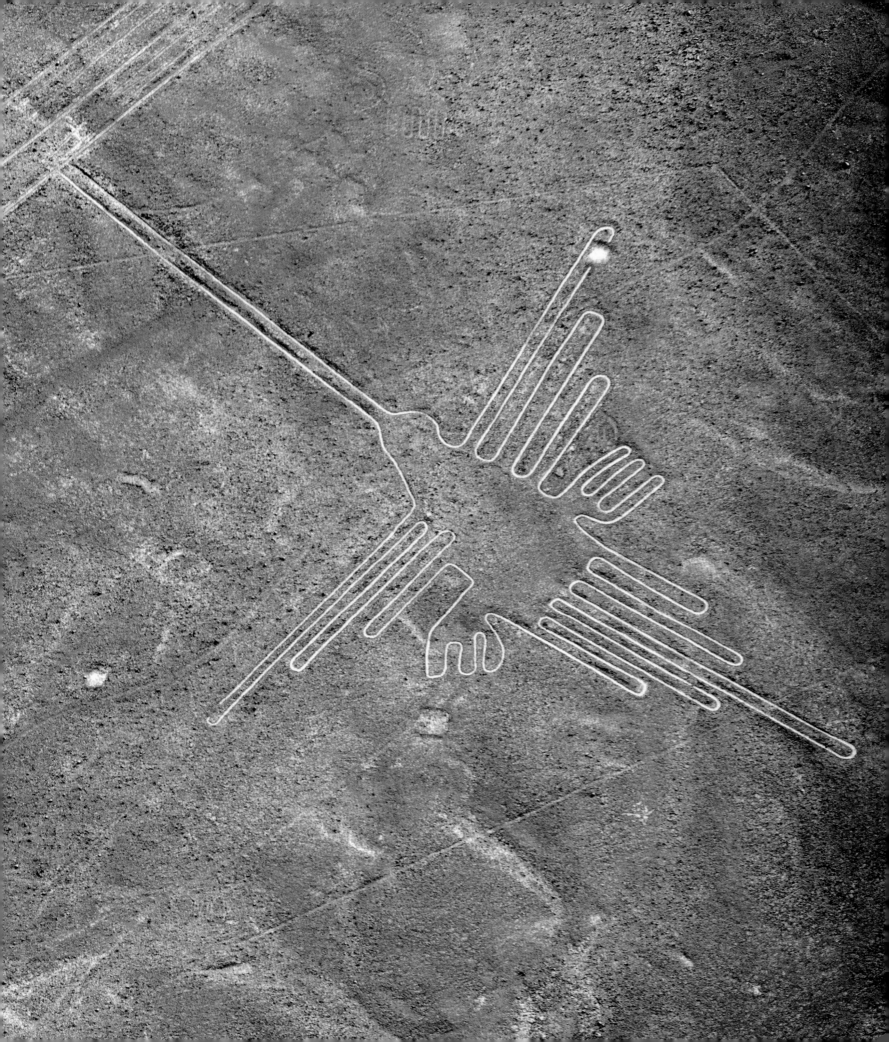

As with so many of the world's most famous monuments it seems unlikely that we will ever be able to do much more than make educated guesses at the purpose of the Nazca Lines, but these vast images, etched into the landscape, continue to fascinate us, pointing, as they do, to secrets that the human race has long forgotten.

*Previous page, left:* An aerial view of the Nazca Plateau, criss-crossed with lines. The longest straight line stretches more than 14.5 kilometers (nine miles).

*Previous page, right:* One of the most famous of Nazca's figures is the Hummingbird, which was also the first seen by Paul Kosok when he flew over the desert in 1941.

*Above left:* A geoglyph representing hands. One only has four fingers, creating yet another mystery.

*Above:* Sometimes known as the Owlman, this human figure—with its bulbous eyes, space-helmet head, and one arm raised to the sky—has been used by some as evidence of contact between the Nazca people and extraterrestrials.

*Opposite page:* An aerial shot that explains why some writers have suggested the lines were created as landing strips for alien craft.

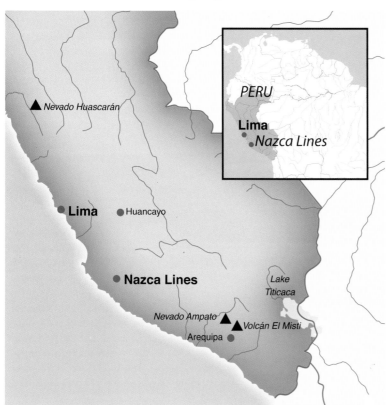

### Site information:

| | |
|---|---|
| **Location:** | Libertadores/Wari Region, Peru |
| **Type of structure:** | Geoglyphs |
| **Area:** | 450 square kilometers (175 square miles) |
| **Completed:** | c. 500 BCE–500 CE |
| **Date of Inscription as a UNESCO World Heritage Site:** 1994 | |
| **UNESCO Criteria:** | (i) (iii) (iv) |

# MACHU PICCHU
## PERU

*Perched on a ridge 2,430 meters (7,970 feet) above sea level between two mountains (Machu Picchu and Huayna Picchu), the astounding city of Machu Picchu is a worldwide symbol of the Inca culture and represents a phenomenal level of engineering and architectural skill.*

A TRULY RARE—AND LUCKY—INCAN CITY, during the mid-sixteenth century Spanish Conquest the invaders failed to discover the location of Machu Picchu and it escaped the widespread destruction visited on the Incan culture by the conquistadores.

One of the youngest sites in this book, and one of the most beautiful, it was constructed around 1450—probably as an estate for the Incan king, Pachacuti (1438–72), although other theories have suggested that it might have served as a scientific station for creating new crops, as a women's retreat, or even a prison. Machu Picchu's position would have made the citadel easy to defend in the event that any invader discovered its location, while it was only 80 kilometers (50 miles) from the capital at Cusco. Bounded on three sides by the Urubamba River that loops

*Above:* The Intihuatana stone (sometimes known as the Inti Watana or Hitching Post of the Sun) is a puzzling object aligned to the cardinal points of the compass. No one knows what it was used for or what spiritual significance it might have.

*Left:* A view over the lower section of the city, which would have been used by agricultural workers.

*Right:* The view across the city towards the distinctive peak of Huayna Picchu.

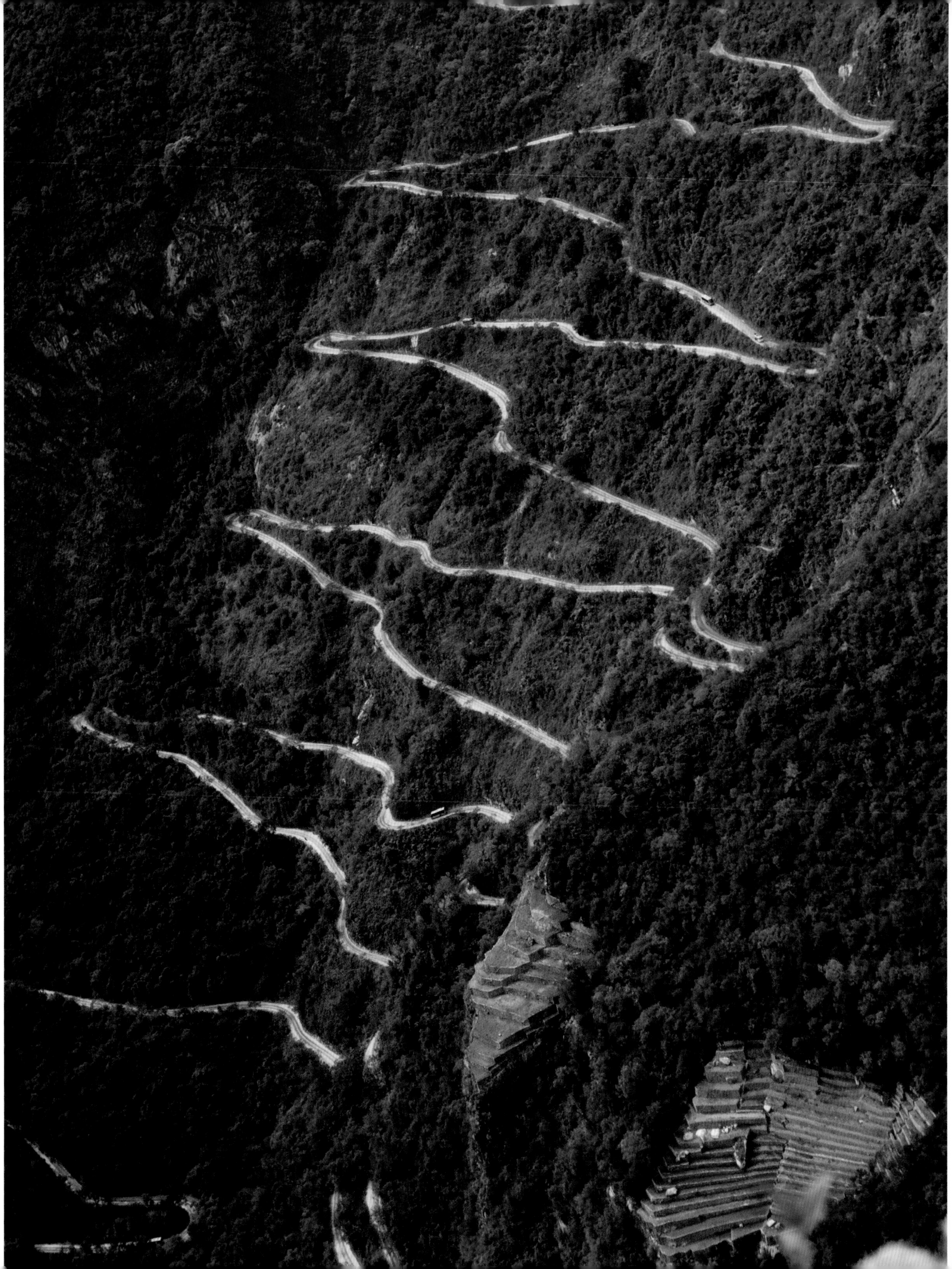

PERU

Nevado Huascarán ▲

Lima

Machu Picchu

● Lima

● **Machu Picchu**

● Cusco

*Lake Titicaca*

through the valley below and with sightlines to important mountains, it is also possible that the site was chosen for spiritual reasons associated with the landscape.

The sophistication and expertise involved in raising Machu Picchu was extraordinary and created a city that blends harmoniously with the scenery while altering the topography to meet human needs. Before the city itself was built, the sheer cliff faces of the ridge were meticulously terraced to prevent landslides that might have toppled the city from its lofty perch. These multiuse terraces were filled with sand, chips of stone, and soil to help slow drainage. Taking advantage of the water

*Opposite page:* Hairpin bends in the road that leads up to Machu Picchu. Many visitors prefer to hike to the site, an arduous but spectacular walk.

*Below:* Machu Picchu's Temple of the Sun. Note the semicircular tower (the Torreon), which is thought to have been used as an observatory.

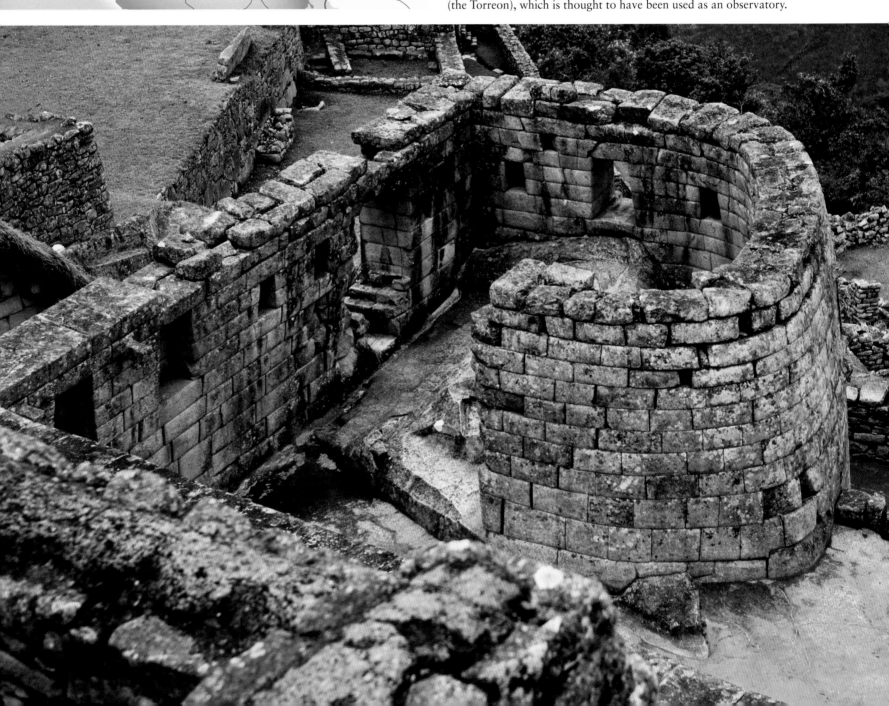

run-off, crops were planted in the terraces and would have produced considerably more food than needed by Machu Picchu's estimated 1,000 inhabitants.

The city itself represents an equally impressive level of engineering know-how. It contains around 200 buildings and is split into two, arranged around a central square (which also helped stabilize the terrain) with around 3,000 steps linking the many levels of the steep metropolis. The buildings were constructed of perfectly cut stones that were quarried on site and fitted together without mortar in a fashion that would have helped prevent earthquake damage (the city sits on two fault lines). The higher part of the city contains three distinct areas: a residential area, a district set aside for royal use, and a sacred section containing temples and an observatory. Elsewhere the lower part of the city is thought to have comprised an agricultural zone, containing warehouses.

Among the upper city's treasures is an object that has puzzled archaeologists for generations. The Intihuatana (known popularly as the

Hitching Post of the Sun) is a large piece of carved granite. Topped with a flat, four-sided shape that aligns to the cardinal points of the compass (like the sides of the Great Pyramid at Giza) it also features a protrusion that indicates magnetic north, as well as a step that might have been used as an altar. Most experts believe that the stone served as a sundial and calendar while others suggest that it may have had astronomical or spiritual significance for a culture that revered the landscape: Intihuatana also aligns with important mountains in the region.

Machu Piccu's most important religious structure is thought to have been the Temple of the Sun, which features an interesting semicircular tower (the Torreon) that is thought to have been a solar observatory. At its foot is a passage that leads down into an underground cave where the mummies of royals may have been housed (rather than placing their mummified kings in tombs as the Egyptians did, the Incans displayed them and treated them as if they were still living). Other sacred buildings include the superb Temple of Three Windows, oriented to the sunrise and with windows representing the division of the Incan

spiritual world into realms of the sky, earth, and inner world. Here, there are also the scratched names of three men, dated July, 1902—nine years before the celebrated explorer, Hiram Bingham III (1875–1956), "discovered" Machu Picchu and brought it to the attention of the world.

Machu Picchu was abandoned around 1570, for reasons that remain unclear. It is thought possible that European diseases ravaged the Incan people as the Spanish ravaged their cities. The few remaining inhabitants may not have had sufficient resources to maintain themselves in such an isolated spot and may simply have drifted away. Sadly, the invaders burned or destroyed a huge wealth of Incan learning, which may well have included documents that might have shed more light on the history and purpose of this magical citadel and its temples. Today, it is, unsurprisingly, recognized as one of the New Seven Wonders of the World. Despite the lengthy journey involved, each year it attracts hundreds of thousands of visitors eager to see one of the few sites where the genius and beauty of Incan culture can still be felt.

*Above:* A view of Machu Picchu that gives an idea of how meticulously the site was prepared with terraces to aid stability and drainage before any buildings were raised.

### Site information:

| | |
|---|---|
| **Location:** | Cuzco Region, Peru |
| **Type of structure:** | City, temple, and palace complex |
| **Area:** | 380 square kilometers (150 square miles), including protected surrounding areas |
| **Completed:** | c. 1450 CE |

**Date of Inscription as a UNESCO World Heritage Site:** 1983

**UNESCO Criteria:** (i) (iii) (vii) (ix)

# TEOTIHUACAN
## MEXICO

*Probably originally settled between 400 and 150 BCE, the city of Teotihuacan in modern-day Mexico was once the Rome of Mesoamerica.*

TEEMING WITH PEOPLE AND FAMED FOR THE SKILL AND CREATIVITY OF ITS ARTISANS, its influence was felt for thousands of miles, inspiring distant craftsmen and builders to emulate its wonders. Strangely, this confident and successful people—who felt no need to erect defenses around their city—left little behind them save the remains of their incredible city and questions. No one today knows for sure who the great pyramid builders of Teotihuacan were, where they came from or where they went, or even what they called themselves.

Though the Mayans may have referred to it as "puh" (the place of reeds), the name "Teotihuacan" was given to the city by the Aztecs after the city had fallen and means "place where gods were born." It should be noted that none of the names used for Teotihuacan's monuments today were given by its original inhabitants. In fact, there is much that remains unclear about Teotihuacan, but what we do know speaks of a city-state that in many ways was strikingly modern. Home to up to 200,000 people at its peak, it was arranged on a strict grid layout that contained palaces, grand mansions, and residential areas where

people from different parts of the Mesoamerican world would have congregated, forming neighborhoods with distinct atmospheres (much as New York City's Harlem and Chinatown have different cultures to Brooklyn). Here people would have lived in multistory apartment blocks similar to those in today's cities. At the city's heart, however, lay a monumental center completely alien to modern cities, and one that was literally out of this world.

Possibly laid out to symbolize the universe, the cultural and spiritual center of Teotihuacan was arranged along a wide avenue (now known as the Street of the Dead) that was lined with smaller platforms as well as the city's great monuments. Although the theory has not been accepted into mainstream archaeology, some researchers have suggested that the street may once have been filled with water, forming a massive reflecting pool. It was built to align 15.5 degrees east of North, directly pointing to the highest mountain in the region (a common feature at Mesoamerican sites), though the alignment may also have had symbolic resonance for the builders, celebrating a significant day in their calendar.

Interestingly, on 13 August—the day the world began for many Mesoamerican cultures—the sunset lines up perfectly with the Pyramid of the Sun.

At the avenue's head lies the massive, stepped Pyramid of the Moon, which rises to 43 meters (140 feet), and measures 130 x 156 meters (426 x 511 feet) at the base. Facing the Street of the Dead, steps lead up to a ceremonial plateau where it is thought that rituals honoring the great Goddess of Teotihuacan were performed. Dating back to the earliest days of the city, the pyramid was renovated and enlarged six times before taking its final form. Archaeologists have revealed a number of tombs within its precincts, containing human and animal remains (thought to have been sacrificial victims) as well as jewelry and other artefacts that display the skill of the city's artisans.

Further along the Street of the Dead is the colossal Pyramid of the Sun. Measuring 220 x 230 meters (720 x 760 feet) and reaching a height of 65 meters (216 feet), it is the world's third largest pyramid and, like the Great Pyramid of Giza, it represents secrets that no one has

*Previous page:* The Pyramid of the Moon. Steps lead up to a platform at the summit where rites connected to the city's Great Goddess were performed.

*Above:* The view down the Avenue of the Dead from the Pyramid of the Moon. To the left is the Pyramid of the Sun.

*Right:* Carved stone details from steps that lead to the summit of the Pyramid of the Feathered Serpent.

been able to fathom. For instance, the pyramid's summit was once covered with a thick sheet of energy-conducting granulated mica that was brought to the site from a quarry thousands of kilometers away. Removed and sold in the early twentieth century, its purpose remains a mystery.

At the end of the Street of the Dead is the compound known as the Ciudadela (the Citadel), large enough to hold up to 100,000 people and containing a number of monuments as well as the site's third largest pyramid, dedicated to the Feathered Serpent. (Named Quetzalcoatal by the later Aztec civilization, the feathered serpent was a major deity among the Mesoamerican peoples.) Standing over a tomb that contains more than a hundred human sacrificial victims, the pyramid is also the site of a major recent archaeological find. In 2003, torrential rains washed away dirt to reveal a hole at the foot of the pyramid. It led down into a network of undisturbed tunnels and tombs.

Working with meticulous care, archaeologists from Mexico's National Institute of Anthropology and History have so far recovered more than 75,000 artifacts including stone figures, jewelry, weapons, and jars still containing 1,800-year-old corn. Unexpectedly, the dig found substantial amounts of mercury as well as reflective pyrite that had been carefully placed in the walls and ceilings of the passages, creating a star-strewn night sky that may have had important symbolic significance. Exploration and evaluation is an ongoing process but it is hoped that the discovery may shed more light on Teotihuacan's enigmatic history.

The city was abandoned sometime during the seventh or eighth centuries, possibly as a result of ecological catastrophe or war, though there is evidence that the city center was set ablaze during an internal uprising. Nobody knows what happened to the survivors of the cataclysm that befell Teotihuacan, though the legacy of the city's great architects can be seen across the ancient Mesoamerican world.

*Opposite page:* An aerial view of Teotihuacan's center. The Pyramid of the Moon stands at the end of the Avenue of the Dead. Top right is the Pyramid of the Sun.

*Left:* A carving discovered during excavations at the Pyramid of the Moon. No one knows who built Teotihuacan, but its people possessed remarkable architectural and artistic skills.

*Below left:* This piece, also unearthed at the Pyramid of the Moon, is a representation of Huehueteotl, the god of fire who was usually depicted as an elderly man.

### Site information:

| | |
|---|---|
| **Location:** | 40 kilometers (25 miles) northeast of Mexico City, Mexico |
| **Type of structure:** | Ancient city and spiritual complex |
| **Area:** | 36 square kilometers (14 square miles) |
| **Completed:** | c. 200 BCE–c. 750 CE |
| **Date of Inscription as a UNESCO World Heritage Site:** | 1987 |
| **UNESCO Criteria:** | (i) (ii) (iii) (iv) (vi) |

# CHICHEN ITZA
## MEXICO

*Mayan civilization began around 2000 BCE and—probably influenced by the architectural and artistic legacy of the people who built Teotihuacan—flourished into a golden age around 250–900 CE.*

WITHIN CITY-STATES THAT SPREAD ACROSS SOUTHERN MEXICO AS WELL AS TODAY'S GUATEMALA, BELIZE, HONDURAS, AND EL SALVADOR, the Mayans took Mesoamerican culture to new heights, developing a sophisticated writing system of hieroglyphs as well as becoming highly skilled in astronomy and mathematics. They also became masters of other essential arts of civilization, namely creating trading routes, perfecting agriculture, and building fabulous cities.

The best-known city today is, undoubtedly, Chichen Itza. Established around 450 CE, the city's name means "at the mouth of the well of the Itza," a reference to the nearby Sacred Cenote—a huge sinkhole where men and children were sacrificed during times of drought. At Chichen Itza, the Mayans raised a monumental city, boasting great temples, administrative palaces, an astronomical observatory, a court for their favorite (and deadly) ball game, and even steam baths.

At the center of the city was the stepped pyramid known today as El Castillo (The Castle). Dedicated to the god Kukulkan (as the Mayans called the feathered or plumed serpent), the pyramid was built over an older structure—which was excavated in the 1930s and found to contain a room still featuring a throne in the shape of a stylized jaguar. The pyramid rises 30 meters (98 feet) and measures 55 meters (181 feet) to each side at the

base. Decorated with carved serpent heads, each face of the pyramid features a stairway that leads to the monument's crowning temple. While not the largest pyramid in Mexico, its construction demonstrates the incredible cunning of its architects. In the late afternoon of the spring and fall equinoxes, sunlight hits the northwest corner of the pyramid at an angle that throws a moving shadow onto the western stairway balustrade—this shadow cleverly creates the impression of a snake undulating down the pyramid. The building also has strange acoustic qualities, notably transforming a handclap at the base into echoes that mimic the chirp of a bird.

Known as the Temple of Warriors, the second of Chichen Itza's stepped pyramids is an equally imposing structure flanked on its south and west faces by 200 carved columns, which were once painted and supported a vast roof. A broad stairway leads up the pyramid to where a reclining Chacmool statue awaits at the summit. The figure's stomach is flat and during ritual ceremonies a bowl would have been placed on it to receive the sacrificial offering of human hearts. Nearby lies the Osario Pyramid, a smaller example that stands over a natural cave

that was found to contain the skeletons of sacrificial victims as well as offerings of jewelry when it was explored in the nineteenth century.

To the east of the Temple of Warriors is the Great Ball Court. Measuring 168 x 70 meters (551 x 230 feet), it was used for the game known as "pitz" or "pok-ta-pok" by the Mayans, which involved passing a bruisingly heavy solid rubber ball among players without using either hands or arms. The pitch is bordered by two platforms that stand 8 meters (26 feet) above the playing area. Each features a ring of twined serpents where "goals" would have been scored, as well as decorative reliefs of the game, including a grisly depiction of decapitation—the reward of the winning captain whose true prize was a victorious passage to the realm of the gods.

In the southern area of the city is the administrative building named La Monjas (the nunnery) by the Spanish invaders who based their regional capital here, as well as a small temple decorated with masks. Both buildings are adorned with hieroglyphs that have provided archaeologists with clues about Chichen Itza's history. Close by is the semi-ruined but still modern-looking astronomical observatory called El

*Previous page, left:* Chichen Itza's Sacred Cenote sinkhole where offerings were made. When dredged the cenote was found to contain seventy-eight human skulls, of which the majority belonged to adult men and children.

*Previous page, right:* The most famous of Chichen Itza's monuments is undoubtedly the pyramid known as El Castillo.

*Above left:* The Temple of Warriors is flanked on two sides by rows of columns. The existing temple was built over an earlier structure known as the Temple of Chac Mool.

*Above:* Chichen Itza's Great Ball Court is the biggest and best preserved of the thirteen courts that still exist across Mesoamerica.

*Left:* Twined serpents surround the "goal" ring on the wall of the Great Ball Court.

Caracol (The Snail). Sitting atop a stepped terrace, the circular building allowed Mayan sky watchers a view of the heavens uninterrupted by the surrounding vegetation. It features numerous sightlines that were used for tracking the path of celestial bodies, most notably Venus.

Among the site's other structures are mansions for the city's nobility and several stone platforms, including one decorated with reliefs of human skulls. It is believed that the skulls of human sacrifices were placed here to be honored by the living. Today, the site is still being uncovered by archaeologists who hope to understand more of Chichen Itza's fascinating history: not least a reason for its decline in the thirteenth century. Although it was never fully abandoned, the city's heyday ended around this time. The city never faded completely from memory though. Occupied by the Spanish, it later became part of a ranch but was brought to international attention in 1843 when it featured in a book called Incidents of Travel in Yucatan by John Lloyd Stephens, which caught the imagination of the Western world. It now receives upwards of a million visitors every year.

*Left:* Known as El Caracol (because of its interior spiral staircase), Chichen Itza's observatory features meticulously arranged sightlines that allowed Mayan astronomers to chart planetary movements. Sadly, because the building is semi-ruined it is not now possible to know all the celestial events they might have measured.

*Below left:* Named the Nunnery by the Spanish because they thought it resembled a convent, this building is part of a complex that features some remarkable stonework.

*Right and Below right:* Elsewhere in the Nunnery complex, facades and the corners of buildings are decorated with distinctive, hook-nosed masks of the god Chac, the rain god.

**Site information:**

| | |
|---|---|
| **Location:** | Yucatan, Mexico |
| **Type of structure:** | Ancient Mayan city |
| **Area:** | 5 square kilometers (2 square miles) |
| **Completed:** | c. 450–c. 1250 CE |
| **Date of Inscription as a UNESCO World Heritage Site:** | 1988 |
| **UNESCO Criteria:** | (i) (ii) (iii) |

# OLMEC COLOSSAL HEADS
## MEXICO

*Now dispersed around parks due to the destruction of their original settings, the colossal stone heads carved by the Olmec people date to the earliest stages of human civilization in Mesoamerica.*

IN FACT, THE OLMECS ARE REGARDED AS THE REGION'S "MOTHER" CIVILIZATION WHOSE DESCENDANTS CARRIED ON MANY OF THEIR TRADITIONS, including human sacrifice and the popular Mesoamerica ballgame played at Chichen Itza.

Ranging in height from 1.47 meters (4.8 feet) to 3.4 meters (11.2 feet) the heads weigh between 6 and 50 tons. Each was carved from stone that was dragged from a quarry more than 100 kilometers (60 miles) away and carved using the most primitive of stone tools. Each colossal stone depicts a different male head, with realistic facial characteristics—some stern, some smiling. Each wears a distinctive helmet. No one knows exactly when they were made. Estimates put the most recent likely date at around 900 BCE, but it is possible that the heads were carved anywhere up to 1,000 years earlier! As mentioned

previously in this book, it is impossible to carbon-date carved stone and the heads have been moved from sites that might have provided contextual data.

Due to the amount of manpower that must have been expended in moving and carving the stones it is thought likely that each depicts an important person—a chief or early king—a theory that is supported by the fact that at least one head appears to have been converted from a monumental throne. It has been suggested that each ruler's throne may have been altered in this fashion following their death, providing a memorial and meaning the new ruler began his reign with a personalized seat of power.

Though little more can be learned from these enigmatic faces, their appearance has given rise to alternate theories. The most persistent dates to the discovery of the first head by

an archaeologist named José Melgar in the 1860s and has since been circulated by others, including Graham Hancock in his popular book Fingerprints of the Gods. Melgar, Hancock, and others suggest that the heads' features do not resemble those of the local people but are African, indicating contact between the Old World and the New long before Columbus's 1492 discovery of the continent. Hancock also points to the existence of statues and masks with Caucasian-type features elsewhere in the Mesoamerican world to support his ideas. Nevertheless, genetic investigation has failed to show any ancient connection between the people of Mexico and Africa, while other researchers insist that local descendants of the Olmecs have exactly the features depicted.

Whatever the truth of such theories, these mysterious heads connect us to a very distant Mesoamerican culture that surely passed on their skill at working stone to descendants who would go on to refine them as they built their incredible cities.

*Previous pages:* Several examples of the Olmec Colossal Heads, each wearing a different expression and headgear. The Olmecs (whose name means "rubber people" in the Nahuatl tongue) lived in the rubber-producing region of the Mexican Gulf and are thought to be the "mother" civilization of Mesoamerica.

*Opposite page:* Between c. 900 and 400 BCE Olmec civilization centered on La Venta. Now covered in grass, the Olmec Great Pyramid there was probably the largest Mesoamerican structure of its time.

*Left:* The were-jaguar appears to have played an important role in Olmec mythology. Known as the Jaguar Cage, this Olmec structure is made from stone beams.

*Below left:* As well as the colossal heads, the Olmecs produced many other stone sculptures including this one which is thought to represent a high priest. The style clearly influenced successor Mesoamerican civilizations.

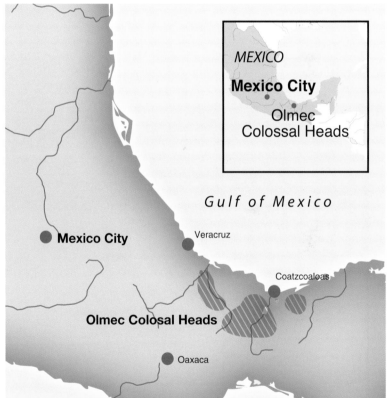

### Site information:

| | |
|---|---|
| **Location:** | Various sites around the Gulf of Mexico |
| **Type of structure:** | Stone carvings |
| **Area:** | Height: Between 1.47 meters (4.8 feet) and 3.4 meters (11.2 feet)<br>Weight : Between 6 and 50 tons |
| **Completed:** | 1500-900 BCE |

# EASTER ISLAND

*Officially belonging to Chile, Easter Island is as far from any other civilization as it is possible to be on this planet.*

SITUATED IN THE SOUTHEASTERN PACIFIC OCEAN, ITS CLOSEST NEIGHBOR IS PITCAIRN ISLAND, 2,075 KILOMETERS (1,289 MILES) DISTANT. Chile itself—the closest mainland country—is 3,512 kilometers (1,289 miles) away. Despite this vast distance, sometime between 700 and 1100 CE the Rapa Nui folk found their way to this remote pinprick of land—a wonder in itself considering their supposed lack of navigation equipment or robust ocean-going vessels. Even more astonishing are the colossal, eerie statues that they left dotted around the island before their culture collapsed.

Known as moai, the 887 great Easter Island "heads" that have been found are, in fact, mostly torsos that end above the knees (although some have been buried to the neck by shifting soil). There are also complete, kneeling, figures. A number of moai, some with representations of the pukao topknot that denotes a chieftain, were placed on specially constructed plinths known as ahu. It is thought that only about a quarter ever made it as far as their intended destination as about half remain at the quarry in the crater of the volcano Rano Raraku. Others seem to have been abandoned in random positions, though these may have been placed to watch over individual clans.

The figures are huge: the tallest, known as Paro, stands 9.8 meters (32.15 feet) high and weighs 82 tons. Interestingly almost all face inland with their backs to the sea. Contextual evidence suggests that their construction took place over a period from about 1100 to 1680 CE, although it is impossible to carbon date worked stone, which has led some to speculate that the moai might be much older.

Each massive statue was carved—usually from compressed volcanic ash, known as "tuff"—with simple basalt chisels and then polished with pumice stone. The rock is comparatively soft and easy to work with basalt tools. One estimate suggests that a complete moai could have been worked by a team of six people over a single year. The statues were probably moved across the island on specially constructed roads by a method of rocking, in a manner that will be familiar to anyone who has ever moved heavy furniture, albeit scaled up. This may have given rise to the islanders' myth that the statues "walked" to their destinations. Shaped coral and dark rock would then have been set into sockets to form vivid eyes. Some, at least, were painted, possibly during elaborate ceremonies to match paints worn by their descendants.

As with many monuments around the globe, the existence of the moai of Rapa Nui has provoked numerous theories. Writers such as Graham Hancock, the best-selling author of Fingerprints of the Gods, have pointed to the their long noses and Caucasian faces, asking why a Polynesian folk

would depict such features on their "ancestors," while pushing forward the idea that the moai might substantially predate the Rapa Nui folk who are supposed to have carved them. Among other geographical peculiarities it has also been shown that Easter Island lies on a straight line around the circumference of the globe that connects the moai to Machu Picchu, the Nazca Lines, the Pyramids of Giza, Persepolis, and Angkor Wat, among other ancient monuments. This is taken as evidence of a global effort to preserve some prehistoric message or culture, possibly connected to a great deluge at the end of the last Ice Age.

The reader may wish to investigate such ideas further, but the accepted history of Rapa Nui is just as fascinating. After a perilous sea voyage of thousands of miles, on simple canoes or catamaran, the inhabitants of Easter Island arrived in the islands around 700 CE, finding a rich habitat easily able to support them. Like other cultures around the world they found that abundance meant freedom from hunting and subsistence agriculture. In turn, this meant they could spend time creating artworks, so the moai are most likely depictions of ancestor-gods whose protection the islanders wished to ensure. Similarly, the Haida people who lived around the area now known as

*Previous page:* A beautiful image of one of Easter Island's 887 moai sculptures at sunset. All but a very few of the statues look inland, suggesting that they may have watched over individual clans or families.

*Left:* These seven moai are unusual in that they are looking out to sea. The site—known as Ahu Akivi—is thought to have had special significance. The seven moai directly face the Spring Equinox sunset and have their backs turned to the Autumn Equinox sunrise.

*Below:* This buried moai is found at Ahu Vinapu, an archaeological site that also features a wall that was constructed in a very similar style to Incan buildings, leading archaeologists to wonder if there was contact between the two cultures.

British Columbia found themselves in an area of natural abundance and devoted much of their time to carving highly stylized and monumental totems.

As time progressed and the population swelled to a height of about 15,000 the island's ecology began to collapse—a phenomenon probably accelerated by the Polynesian rats the colonists had themselves unwittingly introduced, as well as deforestation during production of the moai. A lack of resources led to civil war and the rise of the new religion of makemake, which brought a sudden stop to the manufacture of moai and widespread toppling of existing statues. By the time that Europeans arrived in 1772 the population had dwindled to about 2–3,000, a number that fell to just 111 a century later after European diseases and slave traders had wreaked further destruction. At the same time Christian missionaries worked hard to eradicate the remaining islanders' original culture, meaning that the oral histories that might have given us a greater understanding of the moai were wiped out.

Today, the descendants of those 111 people still inhabit Rapa Nui and the moai are protected by UNESCO conventions as a World Heritage Site. As with so many monuments around the world it is unlikely that the full truth of these magnificent statues with their sombre, profound, expressions will now ever be known. Nevertheless, their artistry stands as a legacy that will last as long as the stones themselves.

*Left:* Almost all of the island's moai were carved from stone quarried here at the Rano Raraku volcano. The landscape is littered with incomplete statues.

*Right:* This moai wears the pukao topknot that is thought to denote a chief.

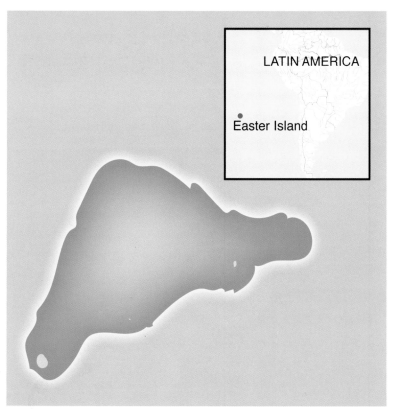

LATIN AMERICA

Easter Island

**Site information:**

| | |
|---|---|
| **Location:** | Easter Island province of the Valparaiso Region, Chile |
| **Type of structure:** | Stone carvings |
| **Area:** | 66 square kilometers (25 square mile |
| **Average height:** | 4 meters (13 feet 1 inch) |
| **Average width:** | 1.6 meters (5 feet 3 inches |
| **Average weight:** | 12.5 tonnes |
| **Completed:** | Tenth to sixteenth centuries CE |

**Date of Inscription as a UNESCO World Heritage Site:** 1995

**UNESCO Criteria:** (i) (iii) (v)

# PICTURE CREDITS